I0816583

Follow us @sacred.scribe.publishing and @evokealchemy
Tag us in your images #SacredScribePublishing
www.sacredscribepublishing.com

Tarot of Oz, Tarot Spread Journal
Published by Sacred Scribe Publishing LLC

Edited by Leah Shoman
Designs by Emma Howard
Illustrations by Emma Howard & Claire Ruby

ISBN: 979-8-9909560-6-3

Printed and bound in China.

All quotes within this publication are sourced from The Wonderful Wizard of Oz book series by L. Frank Baum and are used to inspire and illustrate the themes of this work.

Dorothy: "I've a feeling we're not in Kansas"

Introduction

This Journal Belongs To

....

Greetings, honorary Ozite, welcome to Oz and your enchanting journey through this tarot spread journal.

Step into a world where love, strength, wisdom and courage light your path, guided by the cherished characters of Oz.

Within these pages, discover the tenderness of the Land of Gillikins, the warmth of Quadlings, the clarity of Winkies, and the bravery of Munchkins.

Each spread invites you to dance through these mystical lands, where heart and intuition harmonise, opening doors to profound wisdom and inner truths uncovered.

May your path be illuminated so that you may return home fuelled by the magic that resides within you.

With Love and Light,
Emma

Dorothy: "We must be over the rainbow."

Contents

Wicked Witch: "I'll get you, my pretty."

Contents

Glinda: "Use the silver shoes."

Using Your Journal

This is where you will find the description of the spread you are using.

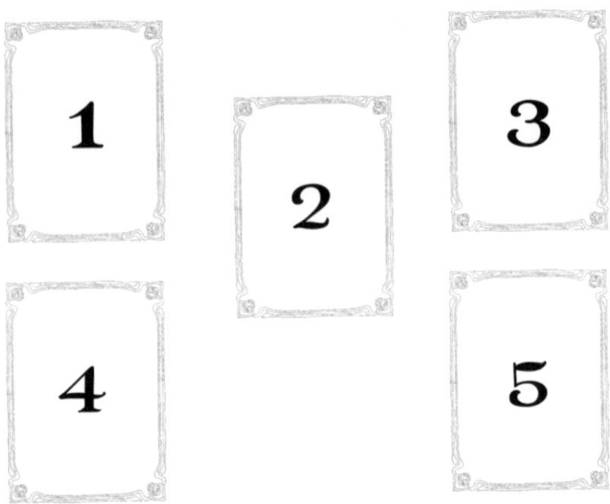

Here will be the basic spread questions

1
2
3

Here you will find the extended spread questions

4
5
6

Date: ....../....../......

An affirmation relating to the spread

i.e I choose to create a day filled with kindness

What deck called to me to be used today?

i.e The Tarocle of Oz Deck

What is my own interpretation of each card?

An area to write your card meanings

i.e Strength - I will move forward today with conviction

Ace of wands - There is potential for great success

Below you will find prompts to follow

What does my higher self believe the message of the reading to be?

i.e I know that I do not take myself as seriously as I could and I should be more assertive

How does this reading inspire me to take action?

i.e I feel supported to make decisions of my own and follow through

Most prominent shadow this reading?

i.e my insecurities, this showed up twice today.

Reflective thoughts & feelings

i.e This spread told me what I knew but was in denial of.

Elemental influence

i.e I mostly had air, meaning I could be overthinking

Venture To The City

Laid in an emerald shape, embark on a journey to the Emerald City, exploring facets of your true self. Delve into what motivates your actions and uncover desires shaping your quest. Revealing personal insights that guide your path forward.

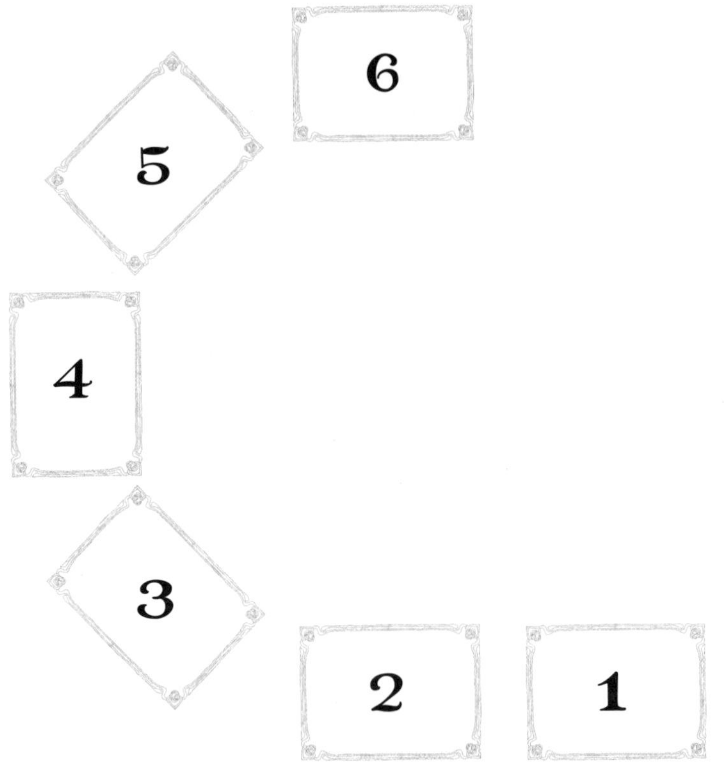

Dorothy: "I shall seek the Emerald City."

Spread questions

1 - What is the core desire driving my current journey?

2 - What underlying purpose do my actions and decisions serve?

3 - What roots or past experiences have shaped my motivations?

4 - What shift is inviting me to step beyond my comfort zone?

5 - What do my relationships teach me about myself and my goals?

6 - What fears or uncertainties must I confront to move forward?

Venture To The City

Navigate through challenges with clarity, allowing discoveries to illuminate your way to the City. Embrace lessons learned, as wisdom deepens your understanding. Let these insights empower your journey and future decisions.

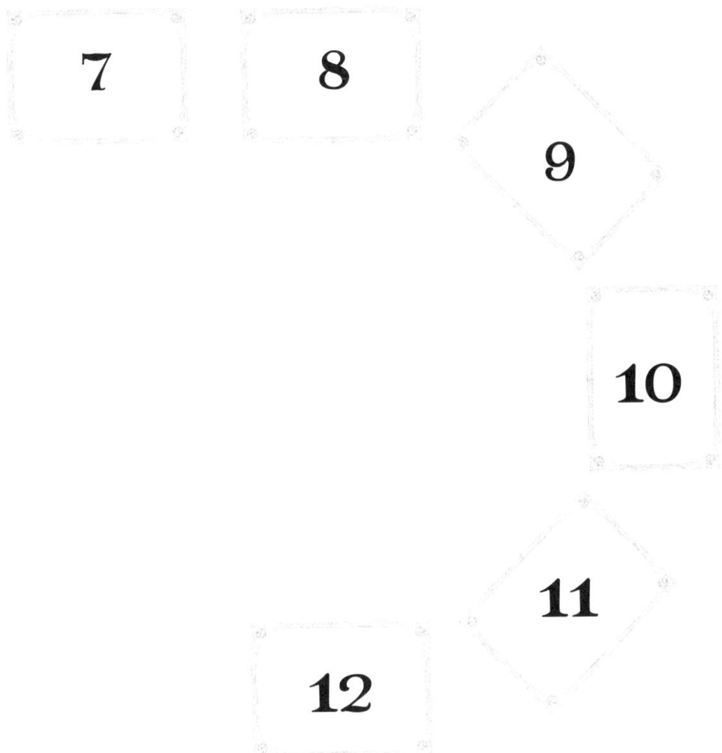

Dorothy: "We're off to see the Wizard."

Spread questions

1 - What talents or abilities might I be underestimating in myself?
2 - What truth about myself am I ready to acknowledge or reveal?
3 - How can my brilliance guide my journey toward fulfilment?
4 - What distractions should I release to see clearly?
5 - What outcome or realisation is my journey leading me toward?
6 - How can I cultivate a sense of contentment within myself?

Date: ....../....../......

I reflect on the past year with gratitude and wisdom, transforming lessons into stepping stones for my future journey.

1: ....

....

2: ....

....

3: ....

....

4: ....

....

5: ....

....

6: ....

....

What lessons from this past year have brought me strength and growth?

....

My Reflections on the journey of last year	Treasures discovered
....	....
....	....
....	....
....	....
....	....
....	....
....	....
....	....
....	....
....	....

Date: ....../....../......

I discover and embrace hidden strengths, unlocking growth, empowerment and a brighter, more balanced future ahead.

7: ....

....

8: ....

....

9: ....

....

10: ....

....

11: ....

....

12: ....

....

Which challenges did I surmount with ease this past year?

....

Joyous memories to bring into this year

....
....
....
....
....
....
....
....
....
....

What magic words define me?

....
....
....
....
....
....
....
....
....
....

Munchkin Country

Munchkin Country heralds the dawn of new beginnings, where the essence of fresh starts reflects our willingness to embrace change. This land invites us to explore aspects of our lives ripe for renewal and transformation, often hidden behind old routines.

The spreads in this section are designed to gently guide you into the heart of these new paths, encouraging reflection on the potential that awaits and the welcome these changes offer. Embrace how these beginnings can inspire personal growth and openness to new possibilities.

Munchkin Country
Tarot Challenge

Pick one question and one card each morning for ten days.
Reflect upon the meaning and journal your thoughts in the evening.

- What new journey am I ready to embark on?
- How can I embrace change with openness and positivity?
- What fears might arise, and how can I gently ease them?
- How can past experiences guide me in this fresh start?
- Who offers supportive energy in my new beginnings?
- What lessons does this new chapter hold for me?
- How can I create opportunities for growth in this transition?
- What potential do I have yet to discover in this venture?
- How does my mindset shape my approach to beginnings?
- What daily practices will support my journey forward?

Glinda: "Follow the Yellow Brick Road."

Dorothy's Transformation

This spread is designed in a spiral, showing the whirlwind of change that brings new beginnings. Each card represents stepping into transformation with courage and support, mirroring Dorothy's unexpected journey into a world of fresh perspectives and resilient growth.

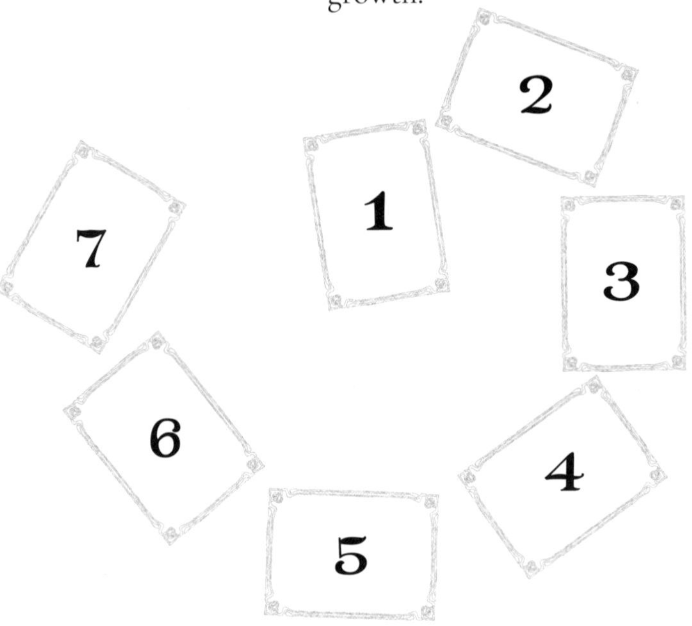

Spread questions

1 - What change has entered my life unexpectedly?
2 - How does this surprising change alter my life's landscape?
3 - Who should I welcome into my journey to help and assist me?

Extended spread questions

4 - Who offers necessary guidance for this unexpected change?
5 - What strength do I need to embrace this change?
6 - What future potential does this change hold?
7 - What first step should I take?

Date: ....../....../......

I embrace change as a catalyst for personal growth and new beginnings.

What deck called to me to be used today?

What is my own interpretation of each card?

How does this reading inspire me to take action?

Most prominent lesson I've become aware of this reading?

Reflective thoughts & feelings

Elemental influence

Welcome to Munchkinland

This spread forms a welcoming circle, echoing the embrace of new beginnings and supportive friendships. Each card invites exploration of the unknown, fostering courage and joy as you embark on journeys, much like Dorothy's warm welcome into Munchkinland.

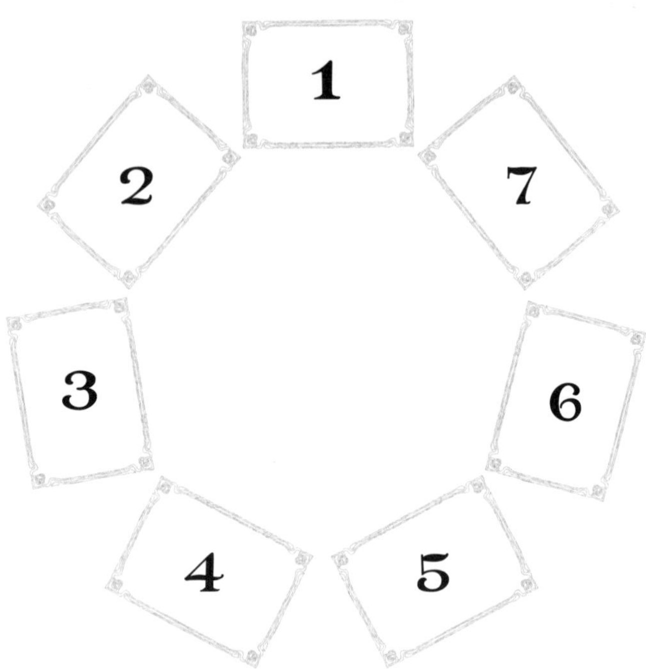

Spread questions

1 - Where am I starting anew?
2 - What unfamiliar path am I being urged to follow?
3 - What magickal guidance should I be seeking at this time?

Extended spread questions

4 - What fears are holding me back from my own true potential?
5 - How can I open up to new friendships to enhance my spirituality?
6 - What joy can I find along this path of enlightenment?
7 - Which present opportunities should I be exploring?

Date: ....../....../......

I welcome fresh starts and open my heart to new adventures and friendships.

....

What deck called to me to be used today?

....

What is my own interpretation of each card?

....

....

....

....

....

....

....

....

....

....

....

....

....

How does this reading inspire me to take action?

....

....

Most prominent lesson I've become aware of this reading?

....

Reflective thoughts & feelings	Elemental influence
....	....
....	....
....	....
....	....
....	....

Path to Possibilities

This spread flows in an arc, symbolising the vast potential and opportunities ahead. Each card guides you to shift perspectives, mirroring the hopeful path Dorothy treads toward limitless possibilities.

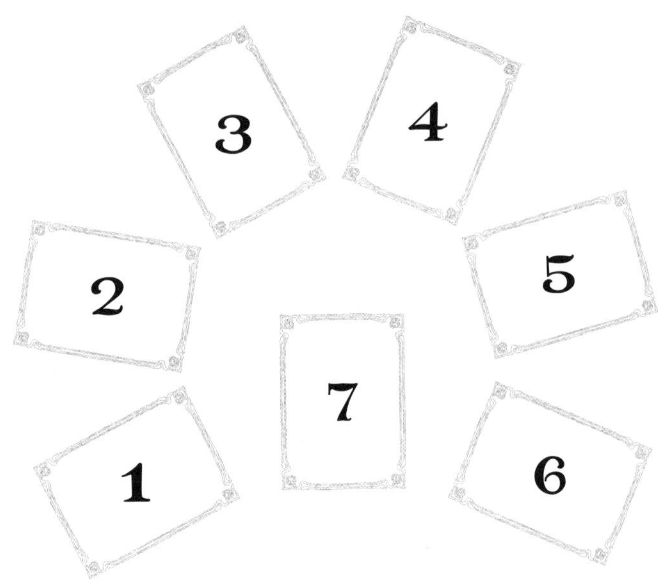

Spread questions

1 - What possibilities are on the horizon?
2 - What should I see from a different angle?
3 - Where can I take proactive steps for inspired initiatives?
4 - Who or what will assist me in navigating these obstacles?

Extended spread questions

5 - What should I explore further in order to foster curiosity?
6 - How can I open my heart to welcome unexpected allies?
7 - What potential outcomes should I focus on at this time?

Date: ....../....../......

I explore new opportunities with hope, seeing limitless potential along my path.

....

What deck called to me to be used today?

....

What is my own interpretation of each card?

....

....

....

....

....

....

....

....

....

....

....

....

....

How does this reading inspire me to take action?

....

....

Most prominent lesson I've become aware of this reading?

....

Reflective thoughts & feelings	Elemental influence
....	....
....	....
....	....
....	....
....	....

Journey on The Road

This spread is laid out in a winding path, symbolising exploration and discovery. Each card embarks on a journey through new experiences and connections, akin to Dorothy's adventures on the road, uncovering insights and growth.

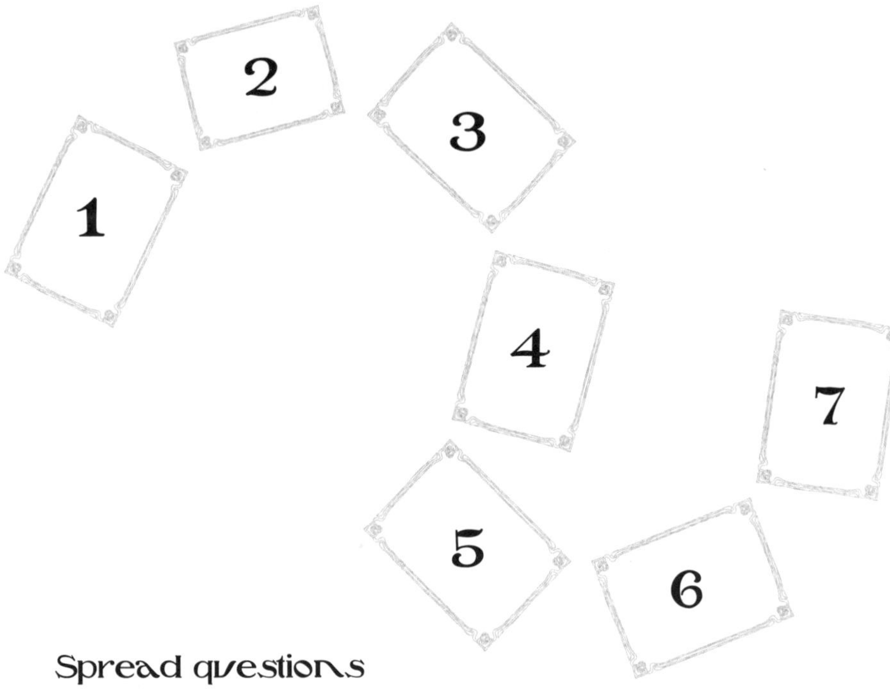

Spread questions

1 - What new beginnings are awaiting me this season?
2 - What unknowns should I embrace on this mysterious path?
3 - Who has a genuine heart and offers kindness and support?
4 - How can this experience encourage emotional growth?

Extended spread questions

5 - What insights should I gain as I make new decisions?
6 - Which relationships will influence my journey?
7 - What dreams should guide my steps along this road?

Date: ....../....../......

I confidently navigate unknown paths, gaining insights to aid my personal growth.

....

What deck called to me to be used today?

....

What is my own interpretation of each card?

....

....

....

....

....

....

....

....

....

....

....

....

....

How does this reading inspire me to take action?

....

....

Most prominent lesson I've become aware of this reading?

....

Reflective thoughts & feelings	Elemental influence
....	....
....	....
....	....
....	....
....	....
....	....

Companions

This spread unfolds in a branching pattern, symbolising the growth of support networks. Each card represents the nurturing of friendships and alliances, reminiscent of Dorothy's journey with her companions.

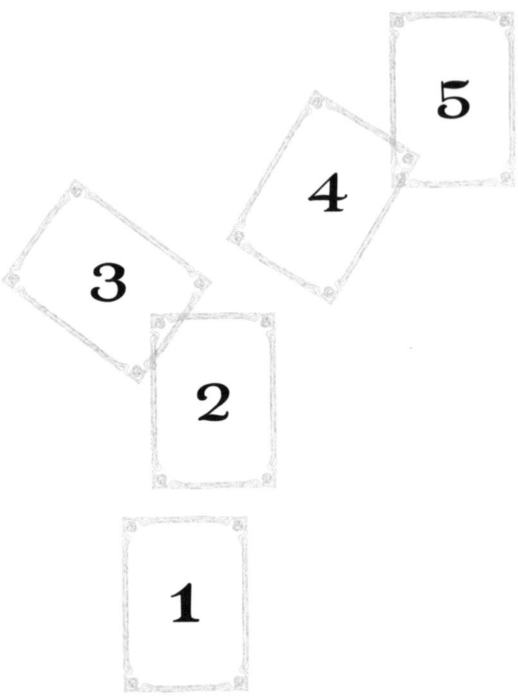

Spread questions

1 - What new person is entering my life?

2 - How can I nurture the connection with this kindred spirit?

3 - How does a sense of community support my connections?

4 - What joint efforts will bring collaborative success my way?

5 - Who should I create new bonds of trust with?

Date: ....../....../......

I build supportive alliances, fostering trust and collaboration on my journey.

What deck called to me to be used today?

What is my own interpretation of each card?

How does this reading inspire me to take action?

Most prominent lesson I've become aware of this reading?

Reflective thoughts & feelings

Elemental influence

Key to Change

This spread forms a key shape, symbolising unlocking transformation. Each card guides embracing change and discovering new strengths, reflecting Dorothy's evolving path through transformative moments.

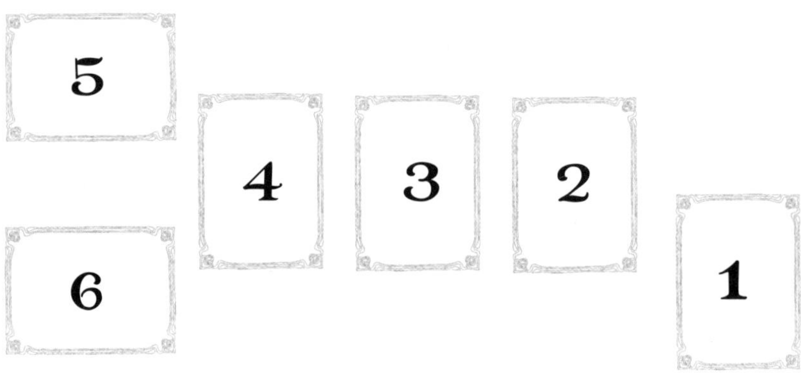

Spread questions

1 - What change will unlock new callings for me to embrace?

2 - What new awareness and understandings are coming to light?

3 - What should begin I let go and accept?

4 - Which internal strengths will serve me?

Extended spread questions

5 - What key to potential lies in this transformation?

6 - How will I celebrate milestones of success?

Date: ....../....../......

I unlock transformation with resilience, embracing new strengths within myself.

What deck called to me to be used today?

What is my own interpretation of each card?

How does this reading inspire me to take action?

Most prominent lesson I've become aware of this reading?

Reflective thoughts & feelings

Elemental influence

Foundation of Friendship

This spread is arranged in a supportive base, symbolising the roots of friendship. Each card explores trust, joy and mutual support, echoing the bonds that strengthen Dorothy's journey.

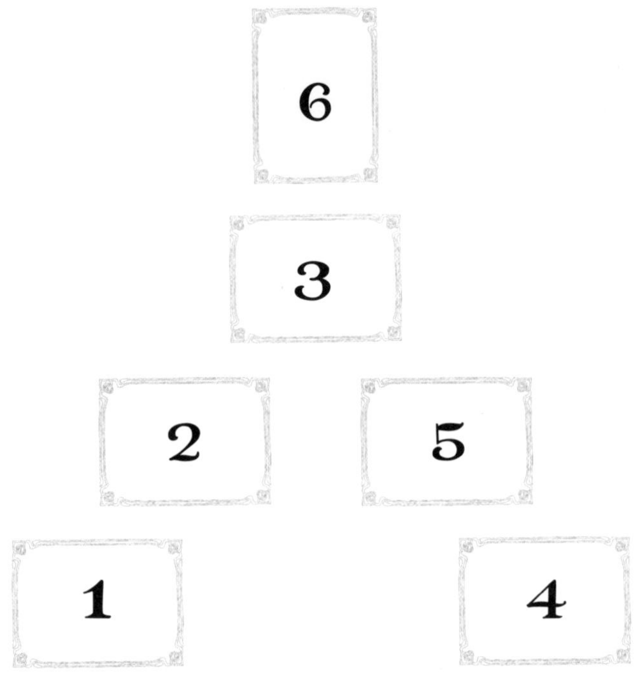

Spread questions

1 - Where am I connecting and finding new friendships?

2 - What mutual support am I giving and receiving?

3 - How can I build and strengthen trust in my friendships?

Extended spread questions

4 - What roles do joy and laughter play in my current connections?

5 - How do these relationships align with my goals?

6 - How can I expand my network of friends?

Date: ....../....../......

I nurture connections with trust and joy, grounding my journey with friendship.

....

What deck called to me to be used today?

....

What is my own interpretation of each card?

....

....

....

....

....

....

....

....

....

....

....

....

....

How does this reading inspire me to take action?

....

....

Most prominent lesson I've become aware of this reading?

....

Reflective thoughts & feelings

....

....

....

....

....

Elemental influence

....

....

....

....

....

Dorothy's New Dawn

This spread follows a rising sun, symbolising the promise of new beginnings. Each card illuminates fresh opportunities and guidance, reflecting Dorothy's journey into uncharted territories.

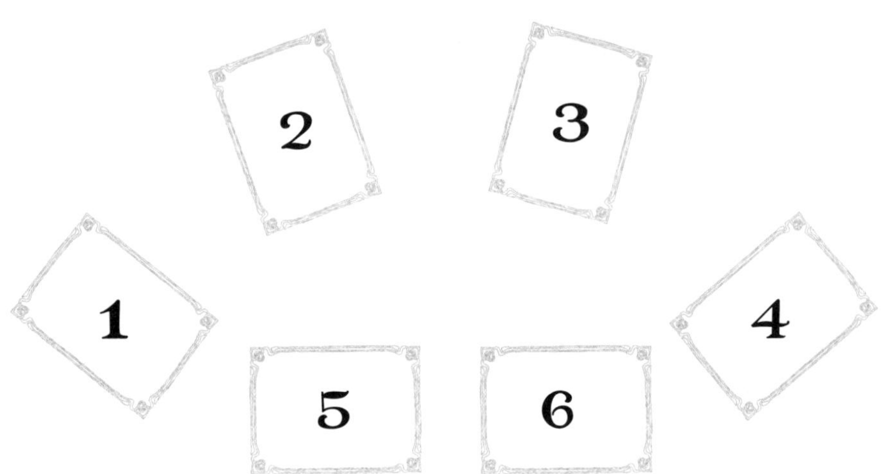

Spread questions

1 - What fresh start is emerging this fine day?

2 - What awakening power should guide me throughout the day?

3 - How do I open my heart and arms to fresh potential?

Extended spread questions

4 - What unexplored paths await as the day unfolds?

5 - How do my actions nurture healthy new beginnings?

6 - What vision am I shaping for my future self?

Date: ....../....../......

I greet each day with optimism, ready to embrace life's boundless opportunities.

....

What deck called to me to be used today?

....

What is my own interpretation of each card?

....

....

....

....

....

....

....

....

....

....

....

....

....

How does this reading inspire me to take action?

....

....

Most prominent lesson I've become aware of this reading?

....

Reflective thoughts & feelings	Elemental influence
....	....
....	....
....	....
....	....
....	....

Sheltered by Kindness

This spread forms a circle of trust, symbolising the warmth of support. Each card explores compassion and encouragement, mirroring the nurturing environment surrounding Dorothy.

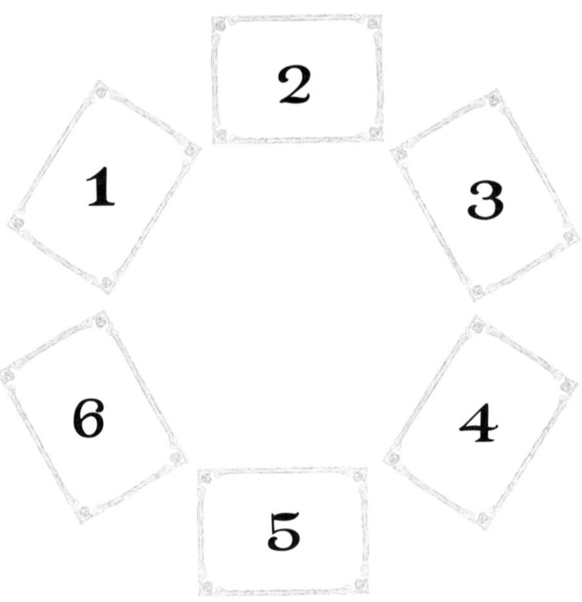

Spread questions

1 - Who provides shelter and comfort to me during times of need?
2 - Where do I draw encouragement from those around me?
3 - What compassionate influence surrounds me?

Extended spread questions

4 - How is support manifesting in my life in unexpected ways?
5 - How does kindness from others influence my actions?
6 - What offers me peace, sanctuary and solace?

Date: ....../....../......

I find strength in compassion, supported by the nurturing kindness around me.

What deck called to me to be used today?

What is my own interpretation of each card?

How does this reading inspire me to take action?

Most prominent lesson I've become aware of this reading?

Reflective thoughts & feelings

Elemental influence

Nurturing Beginnings

This spread forms a bud, symbolising the cultivation of new ventures. Each card embraces growth and resilience, reflecting the nurturing support at the start of Dorothy's journey.

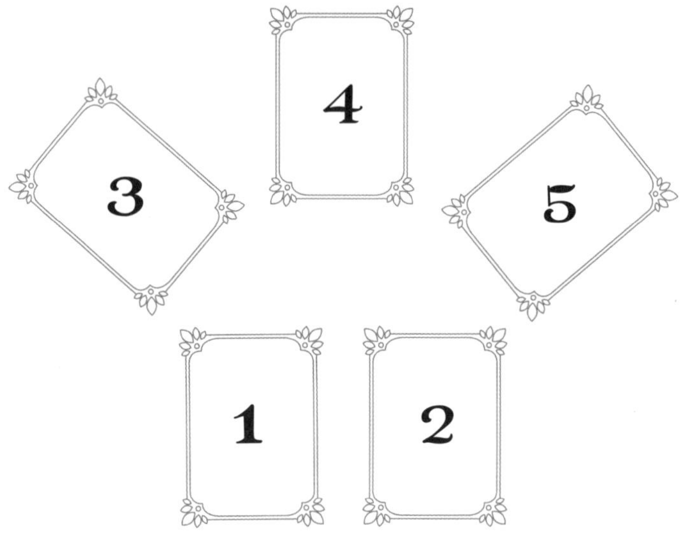

Spread questions

1 - What new seed of potential am I nurturing in my life?
2 - What actions can I take to support this growth?
3 - What is important to foster resilience in my new ventures?
4 - What hopeful visions guide me towards greater success?
5 - What outcomes should I be working toward?

Date: ....../....../......

I cultivate growth with care, embracing the potential of new ventures.

....

What deck called to me to be used today?

....

What is my own interpretation of each card?

....

....

....

....

....

....

....

....

....

....

....

....

....

How does this reading inspire me to take action?

....

....

Most prominent lesson I've become aware of this reading?

....

Reflective thoughts & feelings

....

....

....

....

....

Elemental influence

....

....

....

....

....

Munchkin Wisdom

This spread is arranged in the shape of a Munchkin hat, symbolising the playful guidance and wisdom within. Each card reveals lessons and insights, echoing the wisdom the Munchkins offer Dorothy.

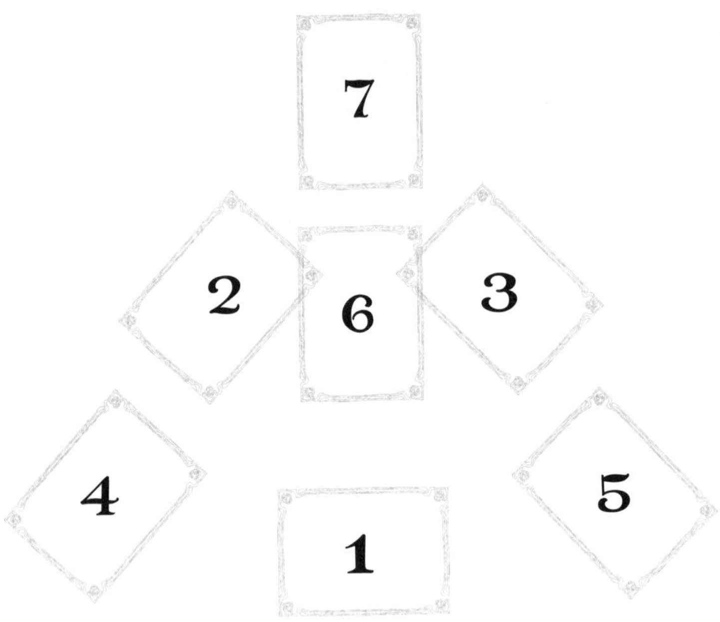

Spread questions

1 - What brand new lessons am I learning anew?

2 - Who offers wise counsel to guide my decisions?

3 - What intriguing insights illuminate my path?

4 - What courage should I summon to broaden my perspective?

Extended spread questions

5 - What knowledge should I pursue to nurture my connections?

6 - What truths are becoming clear to me now?

7 - What path leads to my greatest growth?

Date: ....../....../......

I seek wisdom and learn from every experience, guided by insight and curiosity.

....

What deck called to me to be used today?

....

What is my own interpretation of each card?

....

....

....

....

....

....

....

....

....

....

....

....

....

How does this reading inspire me to take action?

....

....

Most prominent lesson I've become aware of this reading?

....

Reflective thoughts & feelings	Elemental influence
....	....
....	....
....	....
....	....
....	....

Kindnesses Shared

This spread is arranged like a gift box, symbolising the exchange of compassionate acts. Each card highlights how shared kindness enriches connections, reflecting the generosity experienced by Dorothy.

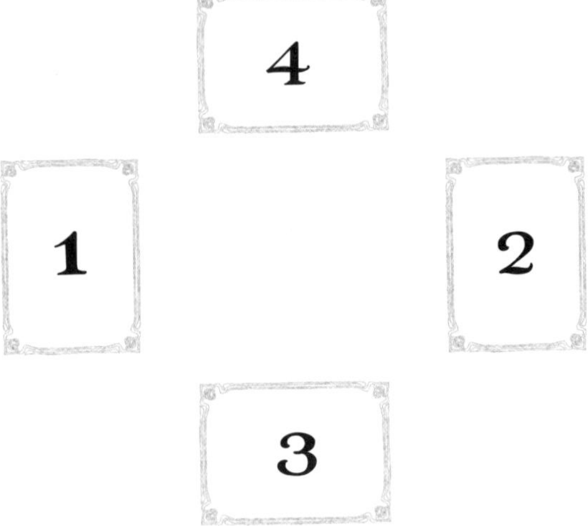

Spread questions

1 - What acts of kindness can I share to help others?
2 - How can I contribute to community joy?
3 - What is exchanged in heartfelt moments between friends?
4 - How does my care and pure heart-centeredness ripple outward?

Date: ....../....../......

I share kindness freely, enriching my life and the lives of those around me.

....

What deck called to me to be used today?

....

What is my own interpretation of each card?

....

....

....

....

....

....

....

....

....

....

....

....

....

How does this reading inspire me to take action?

....

....

Most prominent lesson I've become aware of this reading?

....

Reflective thoughts & feelings	Elemental influence
....	....
....	....
....	....
....	....
....	....

Embracing the Journey

This spread unfolds like an open map, symbolising paths of exploration and discovery. Each card encourages embracing adventure, reflecting the courage and curiosity found in Dorothy's travels.

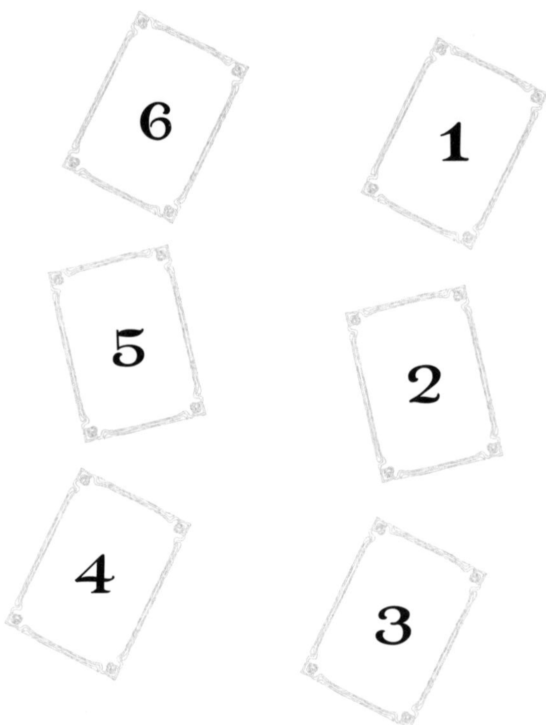

Spread questions

1 - What future pursuit or adventure excites me?

2 - Which paths am I drawn to explore in my lifetime?

3 - How can I align my actions with dreams?

4 - What leaps of faith are needed to propel me toward success?

Extended spread questions

5 - How am I being called to expand my endeavours?

6 - What rewards await this anticipated or fated adventure?

Date: ....../....../......

I embark on life's adventures with courage, guided by my curiosity and heart.

What deck called to me to be used today?

What is my own interpretation of each card?

How does this reading inspire me to take action?

Most prominent lesson I've become aware of this reading?

Reflective thoughts & feelings

Elemental influence

Energised Enthusiasm

This spread radiates like a sunburst, symbolising the vibrant energy fueling new ventures. Each card ignites passion and motivation, mirroring Dorothy's spirited journey through Oz.

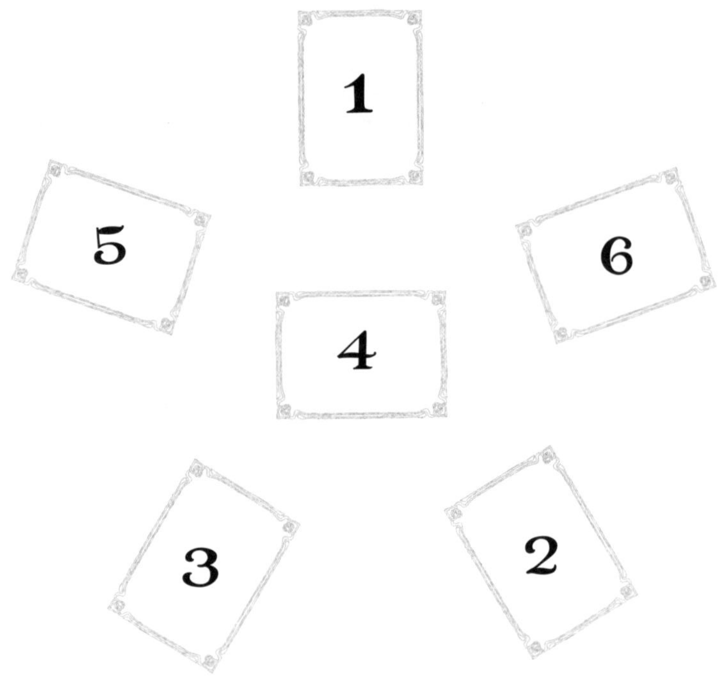

Spread questions

1 - Who or what motivates my life and my choices?
2 - What energies or aspects fuel my passions?
3 - What unexplored roads offer discovery and enlightenment?
4 - How can I embrace enthusiasm when I feel uninspired?

Extended spread questions

5 - What maintains my momentum when life feels flat?
6 - How does my vision for fulfilment and satisfaction manifest?

Date: ....../....../......

I channel vibrant energy into passion and motivation for all life's pursuits.

....

What deck called to me to be used today?

....

What is my own interpretation of each card?

....

....

....

....

....

....

....

....

....

....

....

....

....

How does this reading inspire me to take action?

....

....

Most prominent lesson I've become aware of this reading?

....

Reflective thoughts & feelings	Elemental influence
....	....
....	....
....	....
....	....
....	....

Celebrating Change

This spread is laid out like an open doorway, symbolising entering into new phases of life. Each card explores transformations and growth, reflecting the changes Dorothy embraces throughout her adventure.

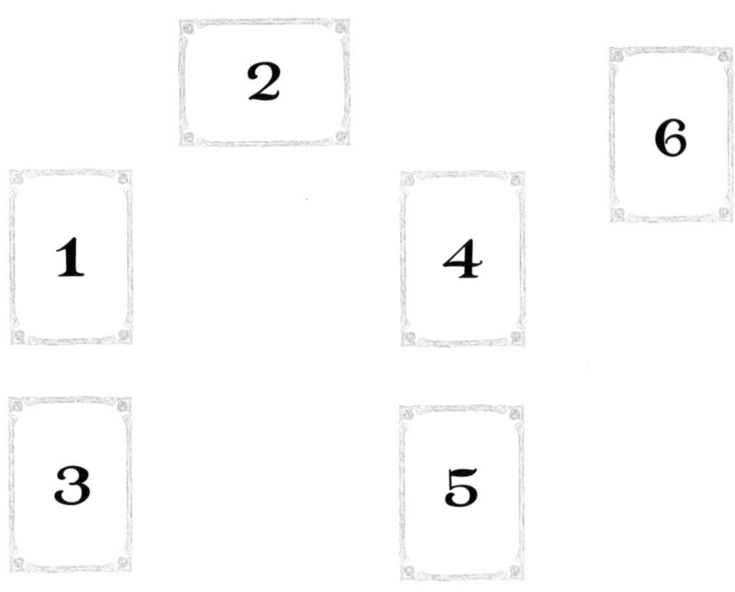

Spread questions

1 - What shifts are moving in that I should look to embrace?
2 - How do I refresh my perspective when I feel blinded?
3 - What milestone is coming that celebrates my success?
4 - How am I transforming into the vision I desire to see?

Extended spread questions

5 - What new horizon appears when I shift my mindset?
6 - How can I find joy in transitional life shifts?

Date: ....../....../......

I celebrate transformation as an opportunity to grow and reach my full potential.

....

What deck called to me to be used today?

....

What is my own interpretation of each card?

....

....

....

....

....

....

....

....

....

....

....

....

....

How does this reading inspire me to take action?

....

....

Most prominent lesson I've become aware of this reading?

....

Reflective thoughts & feelings	Elemental influence
....	....
....	....
....	....
....	....
....	....

Open Arms

This spread is designed in the shape of a welcoming embrace, symbolising the embrace of new possibilities. Each card invites acceptance and openness, reflecting the welcoming spirit that guides Dorothy's journey.

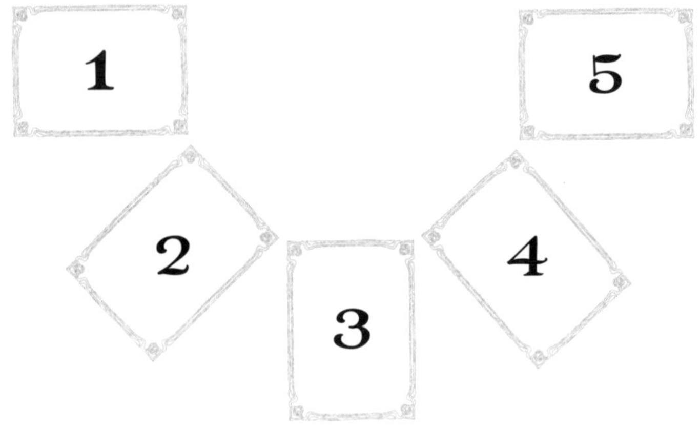

Spread questions

1 - What opportunity is beckoning and inviting me to explore?
2 - How can I express openness to change when I feel resistance?
3 - What random opportunities should I welcome?
4 - What unknowns hold potential in ways I don’t see?
5 - How can I embrace possibility with an open heart and mind?

Date: ....../....../......

I embrace opportunities with an open heart, ready to welcome life's possibilities.

What deck called to me to be used today?

What is my own interpretation of each card?

How does this reading inspire me to take action?

Most prominent lesson I've become aware of this reading?

Reflective thoughts & feelings

Elemental influence

Land Of Blue

As you step into the Land of Blue, the Munchkins guide you to draw a tarot card, this symbolises a new beginning entering an area of your life. Briefly delve into this fresh path and write or draw your reflections on the symbolism of this card.

Date: ....../....../......

I embrace new beginnings with open arms, supported by love and community.

What form of creative expression did I choose today, and what drew me to it?

What elements of the card resonate most with your current journey?

How does the energy of this card inspire you to embrace new opportunities?

Visualise the outcome, how does the card's imagery guide this vision?

What fears or challenges might arise as you embark on this fresh path?

New feelings aroused

Words of inspiration

Winkie Country

Winkie Country illuminates the challenges we face as transformative opportunities. Here, the spirit of bravery reveals strengths within us that we might overlook or underestimate. This is a journey into discovering resilience and fortitude.

The spreads in this section aim to navigate you through the landscape of challenge, encouraging deep reflection on how courage shapes your responses and empowers growth. Uncover how facing these challenges can lead to personal empowerment and strength.

Scarecrow: "Experience is a pretty teacher."

Winkie Country
Tarot Challenge

Pick one question and one card each morning for ten days.
Reflect upon the meaning and journal your thoughts in the evening.

- What current challenge calls for my courage and resilience?
- How can I nurture bravery in the face of adversity?
- Who or what provides strength in moments of doubt?
- How does this challenge help uncover my potential?
- What fears must I address to progress further?
- How can I reframe this challenge as a path to growth?
- In what ways do my actions inspire others?
- What courage have I demonstrated in past challenges?
- How can this challenge shape my future positively?
- What mantra can I create to empower my journey?

Lion: "Frightened? You're talking to a man!"

Lion's Courage

This spread flows like a single arrow, symbolising the journey of discovering courage. Each card encourages bravery, echoing the Lion's path to finding strength within.

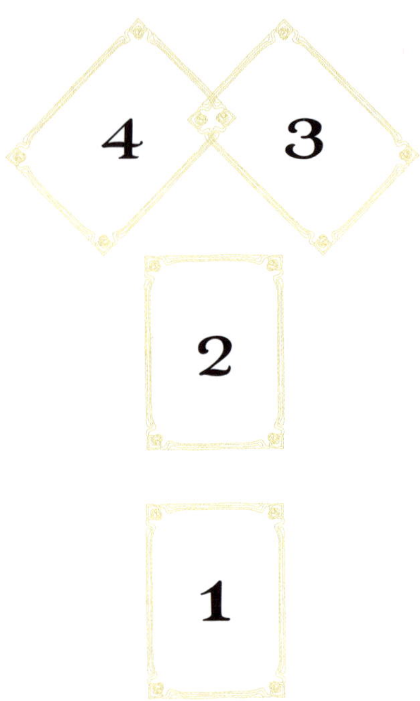

Spread questions

1 - What inner strength am I yet to discover?

2 - What fear am I ready to confront?

3 - Where in life is my courage needed most?

4 - What holds me back from embracing bravery?

Date: ../../....

I embrace my hidden courage, discovering strength in every challenge.

What deck called to me to be used today?

What is my own interpretation of each card?

How does this reading inspire me to take action?

Most prominent lesson I've become aware of this reading?

Reflective thoughts & feelings

Elemental influence

Dorothy's Determination

Laid out like a mountain ascent, this spread symbolises reaching your goals with determination. Each card supports overcoming adversity, mirroring Dorothy's driven steps.

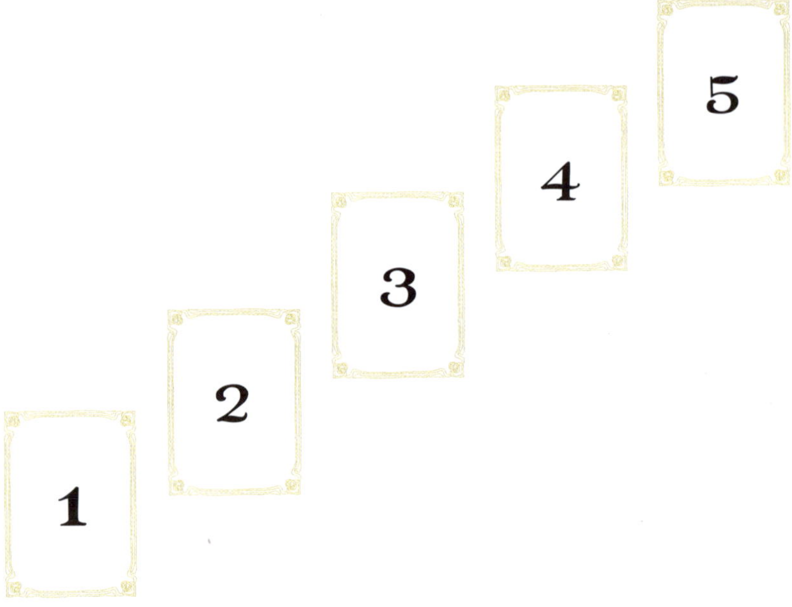

Spread questions

1 - What fuels my determination?

2 - What unseen obstacle stands in my path?

3 - Who provides support and comfort to me during challenges?

4 - How can I maintain focus amid adversity I encounter?

5 - What achievement awaits beyond the challenge I face?

Date: ....../....../......

My resolve is strong, I persevere through all adversity with focus.

....

What deck called to me to be used today?

....

What is my own interpretation of each card?

....

....

....

....

....

....

....

....

....

....

....

....

....

How does this reading inspire me to take action?

....

....

Most prominent lesson I've become aware of this reading?

....

Reflective thoughts & feelings

....

....

....

....

....

Elemental influence

....

....

....

....

....

Tin Man's Heart

This spread is woven like pulsing veins, symbolising emotional growth, life force energy and resilience. Each card uncovers empathy, reflecting the Tin Man's quest for a heart's robust emotional power.

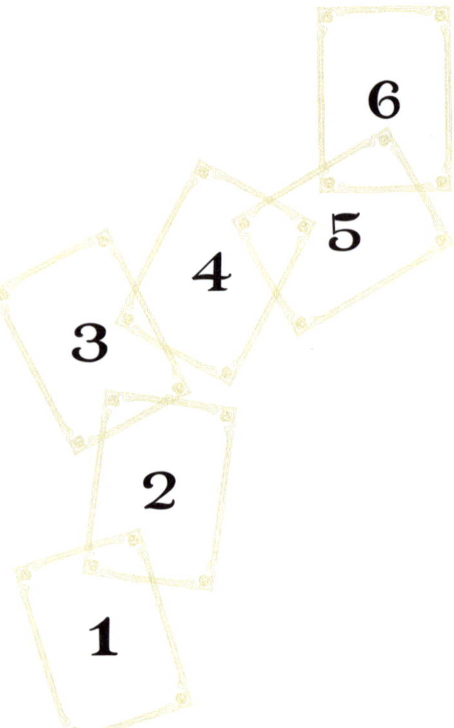

Spread questions

1 - What emotional barrier do I need to overcome?

2 - Where can I introduce more empathy?

3 - What fulfills me emotionally?

Extended spread

4 - What old defences are now unneeded?

5 - How can I use empathy to overcome my fears?

6 - What clarity emerges from my emotional bravery?

Date: ....../....../......

Empathy fuels my resilience, and I embrace heartfelt emotional growth.

....

What deck called to me to be used today?

....

What is my own interpretation of each card?

....

....

....

....

....

....

....

....

....

....

....

....

....

How does this reading inspire me to take action?

....

....

Most prominent lesson I've become aware of this reading?

....

Reflective thoughts & feelings	Elemental influence
....	....
....	....
....	....
....	....
....	....

Scarecrow's Wisdom

This spread unfolds as a branching tree, symbolising insight and problem-solving. Each card helps conquer doubts with knowledge, akin to the Scarecrow's journey.

Spread questions

1 - What knowledge do I possess to help me face challenges?

2 - What confusion must I clear in order to know more?

3 - How can I creatively solve problems to better myself?

4 - What helps me overcome self-doubt that I don't recognise?

5 - What is my next wise step today, tomorrow, this year?

Date: ....../....../......

Wisdom guides my path, dispelling doubt and encouraging growth.

....

What deck called to me to be used today?

....

What is my own interpretation of each card?

....

....

....

....

....

....

....

....

....

....

....

....

....

How does this reading inspire me to take action?

....

....

Most prominent lesson I've become aware of this reading?

....

Reflective thoughts & feelings	Elemental influence
....	....
....	....
....	....
....	....
....	....

Winkie's Resolve

Laid out like steadfast roots, this spread symbolises firm resolve against intimidation. Each card strengthens willpower, reflecting a Winkie's bravery against fears.

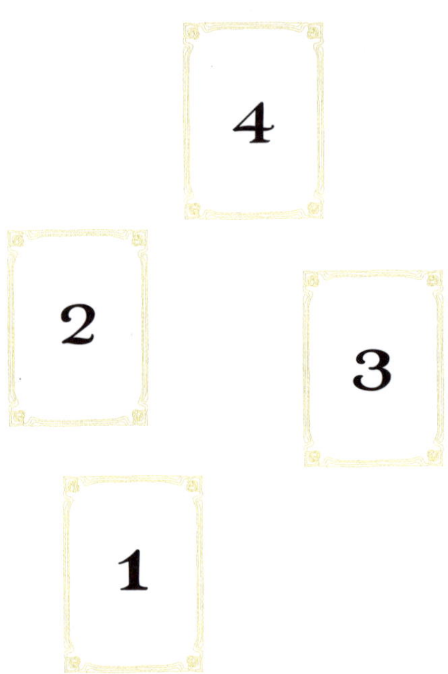

Spread questions

1 - What shadow of wicked intimidation must I face?

2 - What strengthens my inner resolve against intimidation?

3 - How can I liberate myself from fear's grip?

4 - What lies beyond this confrontation with myself or another?

Date: ....../....../......

I stand firm at all times, unwavering in my courage and inner determination.

....

What deck called to me to be used today?

....

What is my own interpretation of each card?

....

....

....

....

....

....

....

....

....

....

....

....

....

How does this reading inspire me to take action?

....

....

Most prominent lesson I've become aware of this reading?

....

Reflective thoughts & feelings

....

....

....

....

....

Elemental influence

....

....

....

....

....

Glinda's Guidance

Laid out like guiding star wand, this spread symbolises wisdom through adversity. Each card illuminates paths with support, echoing Glinda's helpful insights.

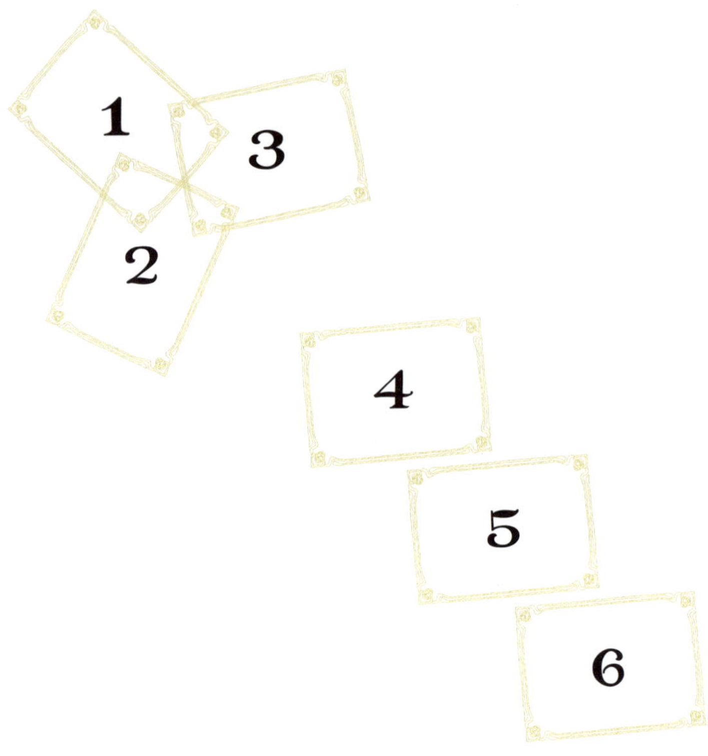

Spread questions

1 - Who or what is guiding me now?

2 - How can I effectively navigate impending storms?

3 - How can I problem-solve effectively when it's required?

Extended spread

4 - What secures my heart strings amidst trials I may face?

5 - What hope guides me forward as a beacon of light?

6 - What blessed opportunity can emerge for me?

Date: ....../....../......

Guided by wisdom, I navigate adversity with clarity and support.

....

What deck called to me to be used today?

....

What is my own interpretation of each card?

....

....

....

....

....

....

....

....

....

....

....

....

....

How does this reading inspire me to take action?

....

....

Most prominent lesson I've become aware of this reading?

....

Reflective thoughts & feelings

....

....

....

....

....

Elemental influence

....

....

....

....

....

Wicked Witch's Bane

This spread arcs like a flying monkey's wing, symbolising defence from personal demons. Each card aids conquering fears, inspired by challenges of the Wicked Witch.

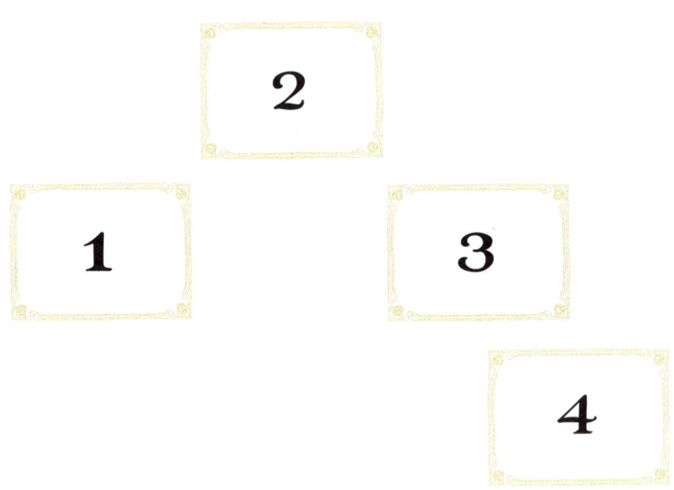

Spread questions

1 - What personal demon needs facing to confront my fears?

2 - What tools do I have for battle against my own will?

3 - Where does my courage break through?

4 - What binds will be broken when I am released?

Date: ....../....../......

I confront my fears, I am empowered by the strength to overcome them.

....

What deck called to me to be used today?

....

What is my own interpretation of each card?

....

....

....

....

....

....

....

....

....

....

....

....

....

How does this reading inspire me to take action?

....

....

Most prominent lesson I've become aware of this reading?

....

Reflective thoughts & feelings	Elemental influence
....	....
....	....
....	....
....	....
....	....

West Wind's Challenge

Flowing as wind gusts, this spread symbolises resilience against resistance. Each card enhances adaptation and strength, inspired by the West Wind's trials.

Spread questions

1 - What gale of resistance holds me back?

2 - What flexible trait of adaptability do I possess??

3 - What advice whispers in my ear?

Extended spread

4 - What fortifies my resolve to take a stand?

5 - What will provide peaceful passage to calm after the storm?

Date: ....../....../......

I know that my resilience and adaptability are my allies in every challenge.

....

What deck called to me to be used today?

....

What is my own interpretation of each card?

....

....

....

....

....

....

....

....

....

....

....

....

....

How does this reading inspire me to take action?

....

....

Most prominent lesson I've become aware of this reading?

....

Reflective thoughts & feelings	Elemental influence
....	....
....	....
....	....
....	....
....	....

Winkie Ally

Formed like a bridge, this spread symbolises alliances for triumph. Each card supports collaboration and support, reflecting the Winkie's friendships.

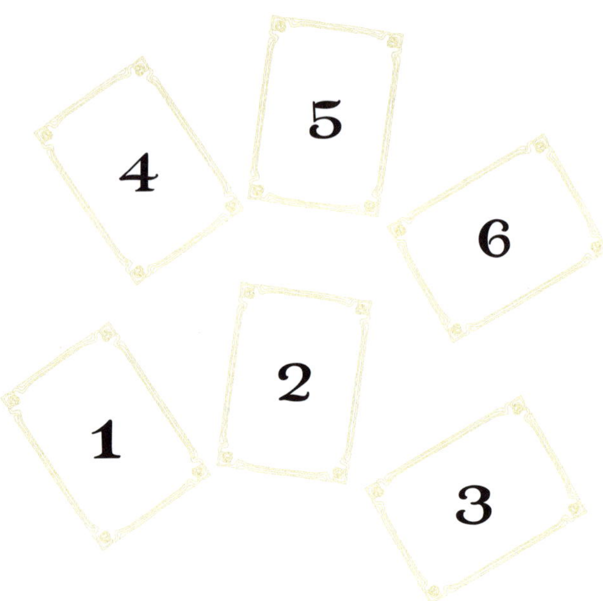

Spread questions

1 - Who is my trusted ally in adversity?

2 - How can unity provide strength?

3 - What shared mission binds us together?

Extended spread

4 - What does each ally bring to this endeavour?

5 - How can I expand my support network?

6 - What shared success is attainable for the collective?

Date: ../../....

I know that together, we are stronger, creating unity in overcoming any trial.

....

What deck called to me to be used today?

....

What is my own interpretation of each card?

....

....

....

....

....

....

....

....

....

....

....

....

....

How does this reading inspire me to take action?

....

....

Most prominent lesson I've become aware of this reading?

....

Reflective thoughts & feelings	Elemental influence
....	....
....	....
....	....
....	....
....	....
....	....

Yellow Brick Test

Arranged like stepping stones, this spread symbolises making progress through critical trials. Each card guides gradual overcoming of obstacles, mirroring Dorothy's path along the yellow brick road.

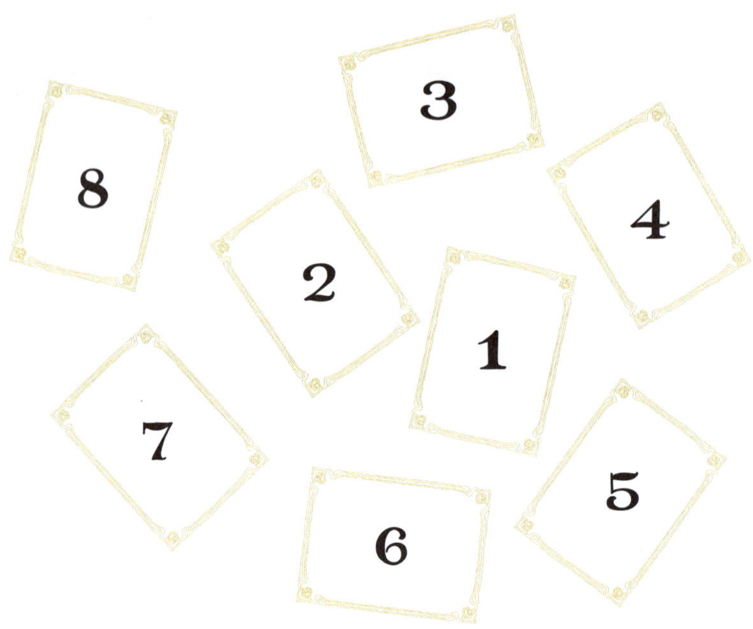

Spread questions

1 - What trials await along my path?
2 - What fear must I encounter and confront?
3 - How can I build my resilience for this journey?
4 - What deceptive paths or false turns should I avoid?
5 - How can partnerships aid my journey?
6 - What inner beliefs will empower my progress?
7 - What challenge will I navigate with ease next?
8 - What victorious reward lies at my journey's end?

Date: ....../....../......

Step by step, I overcome challenges, moving closer to my goals, with ease and joy.

....

What deck called to me to be used today?

....

What is my own interpretation of each card?

....

....

....

....

....

....

....

....

....

....

....

....

....

How does this reading inspire me to take action?

....

....

Most prominent lesson I've become aware of this reading?

....

Reflective thoughts & feelings

....

....

....

....

....

Elemental influence

....

....

....

....

....

Boq's Brave Heart

Shaped like a beating drum, this spread symbolises discovering bravery within. Each card uncovers courage for facing fears, echoing Boq's strong spirit.

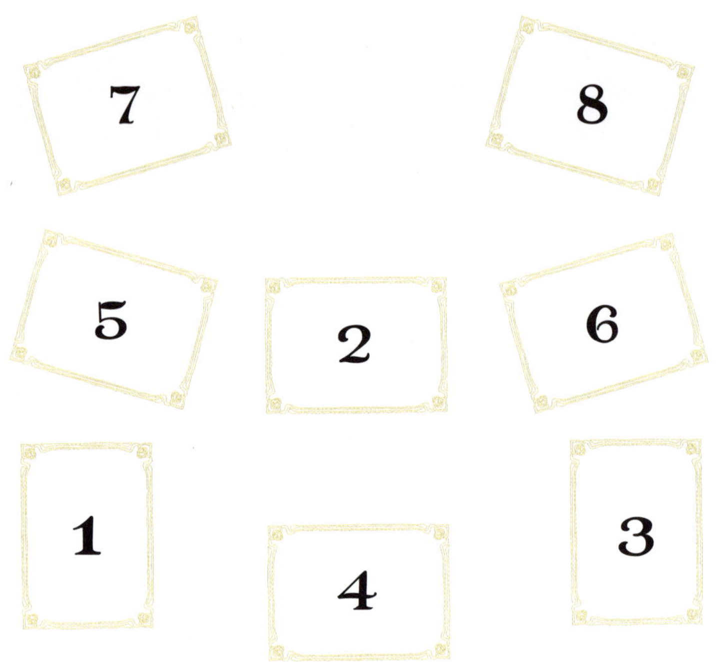

Spread questions

1 - What unperceived strength emerges within me now?
2 - How can I face my shadows and fears with courage?
3 - What energises my fighting warrior spirit?
4 - What ray of hope illuminates my path?
5 - In what ways can I enhance my resilience today?
6 - How can I adapt to changes with bravery and conviction?
7 - Where can I find inspiration to fuel my courage?
8 - What courage remains to be discovered within me?

Date: ....../....../......

My heart beats a brave thrum and I meet life's uncertainties with courage.

What deck called to me to be used today?

What is my own interpretation of each card?

How does this reading inspire me to take action?

Most prominent lesson I've become aware of this reading?

Reflective thoughts & feelings

Elemental influence

Winkie Trials

This spread resembles climbing ladder rungs, symbolising ascending through adversity. Each card reveals resilience and conquering challenges, similar to the Winkie's triumphs.

Spread questions

1 - What adversity is presenting itself to me at this time?
2 - What bold stance do I need to take?
3 - How can the power of persuasion aid my way?
4 - What understanding is key right now?
5 - What core strength protects me?
6 - What triumph emerges for me beyond this adversity?

Date: ....../....../......

I rise through these trials, stronger and more resilient after each ascent.

What deck called to me to be used today?

What is my own interpretation of each card?

How does this reading inspire me to take action?

Most prominent lesson I've become aware of this reading?

Reflective thoughts & feelings

Elemental influence

Forest of Fear

This spread winds like a maze path, symbolising navigating through insecurities. Each card offers guidance to clear fears, inspired by the forest's layered depths.

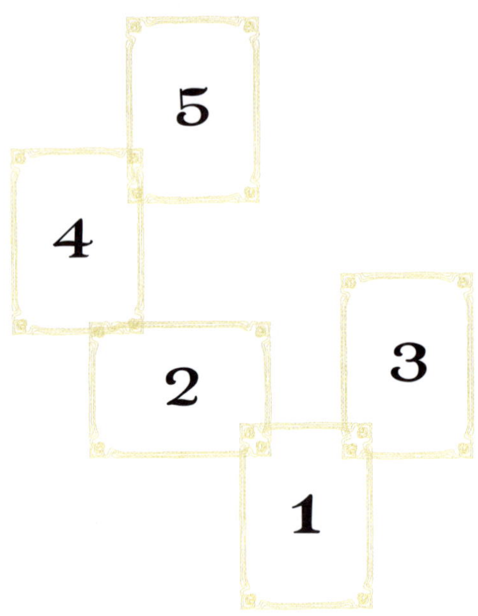

Spread questions

1 - What shadow of insecurity needs addressing?

2 - Where should I courageously step forward?

3 - What in my environment supports my courage?

4 - What fears must not mislead or distract me from my goals?

5 - What new found bravery guides me?

Date: ....../....../......

Insecurity transforms my path, through fear it becomes clear and open.

....

What deck called to me to be used today?

....

What is my own interpretation of each card?

....

....

....

....

....

....

....

....

....

....

....

....

....

How does this reading inspire me to take action?

....

....

Most prominent lesson I've become aware of this reading?

....

Reflective thoughts & feelings	Elemental influence
....	....
....	....
....	....
....	....
....	....

Flying Monkeys

This spread forms a cloud trail, symbolising confronting and taking action towards relentless obstacles. Each card strategizes manoeuvring through trials, capturing bravery.

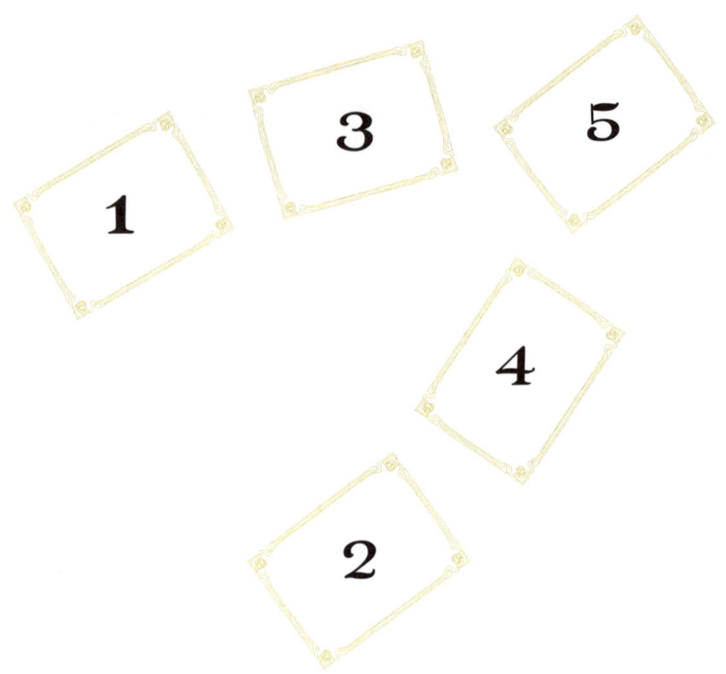

Spread questions

1 - What relentless obstacle do I bravely confront?

2 - Who is my ally and aids me unexpectedly?

3 - What strategic manoeuvre will best serve me?

Extended spread

4 - What resolute action do I need to take?

5 - How will I triumph against the odds with this unpredictable challenge?

Date: ....../....../......

I am agile and strategic, I navigate through life's unexpected challenges fearlessly.

....

What deck called to me to be used today?

....

What is my own interpretation of each card?

....

....

....

....

....

....

....

....

....

....

....

....

....

How does this reading inspire me to take action?

....

....

Most prominent lesson I've become aware of this reading?

....

Reflective thoughts & feelings	Elemental influence
....	....
....	....
....	....
....	....
....	....

Witch's Test

Arranged like a protective shield, this spread symbolises confronting fear with valour. Each card aids overcoming trials, echoing the tests set by the Wicked Witch.

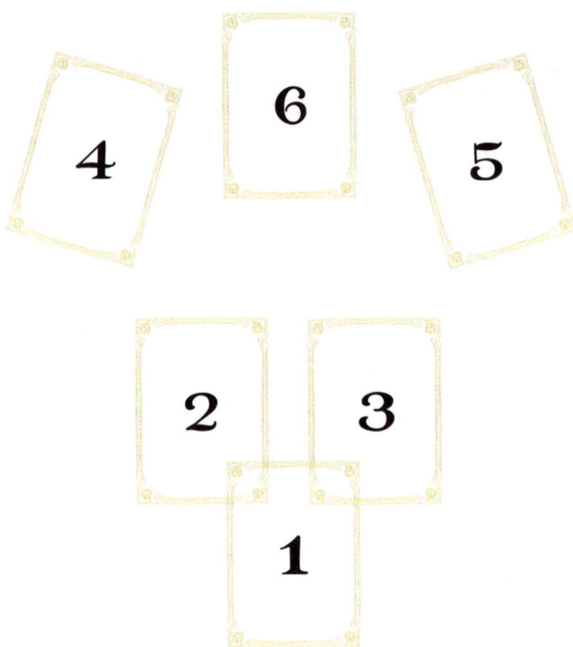

Spread questions

1 - What fearful test, trial or challenge is imminent?

2 - What valour in battle needs unleashing within me?

3 - What solution will help me to overcome this trial?

Extended spread

4 - Who will offer me trusted guidance through the trial?

5 - What is the pathway to defeating my fear?

6 - What achievement awaits for me beyond the test?

Date: ....../....../......

With valour, I face trials, triumphantly, effortlessly conquering each challenge.

What deck called to me to be used today?

What is my own interpretation of each card?

How does this reading inspire me to take action?

Most prominent lesson I've become aware of this reading?

Reflective thoughts & feelings

Elemental influence

Echoes of Triumph

This spread is laid like a trophy of victory, symbolising celebrating conquered fears. Each card highlights inner strength gained, reflecting Dorothy's triumphant journey in the land of Oz.

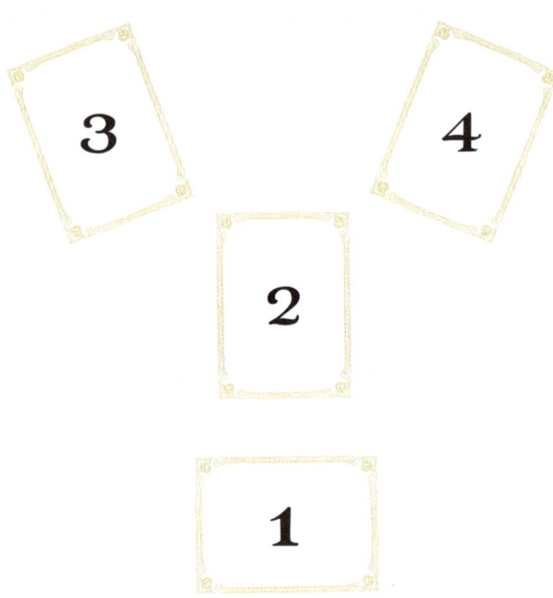

Spread Questions

1 - What fear have I triumphantly conquered?

2 - What strength has emerged and taught me resilience?

3 - What lessons did overcoming the trials bring?

4 - How have I been empowered by my success?

Date: ....../....../......

I celebrate my triumphs with glee! My inner strength echoes my past victories.

....

What deck called to me to be used today?

....

What is my own interpretation of each card?

....

....

....

....

....

....

....

....

....

....

....

....

....

How does this reading inspire me to take action?

....

....

Most prominent lesson I've become aware of this reading?

....

Reflective thoughts & feelings	Elemental influence
....	....
....	....
....	....
....	....
....	....

Land Of Yellow

In the radiant Land of Yellow, the Winkies guide you to pull a card, this embodies a challenge you're facing. Reflect on this obstacle: the courage it demands and the strength you can discover within, and create a spread relating to your journey.

Date: ....../....../......

I face challenges with bravery, discovering strength and courage within my soul.

....

How does the imagery of this card reflect your current situation?

....

....

....

What personal strengths does the card remind you to draw upon?

....

....

....

....

What lessons from challenges of the past can you apply now?

....

....

....

....

....

Describe a potential positive outcome of tackling this challenge.

....

....

....

What is the theme of your chosen spread?

....

....

Chosen Spread questions	Cards Pulled
....	....
....	....
....	....
....	....
....	....

The Dark Forest

Through shadows deep where courage lies, face hidden fears and truths untold. Each twisted tree branch unveils lessons anew, guiding your spirit to strength renewed.

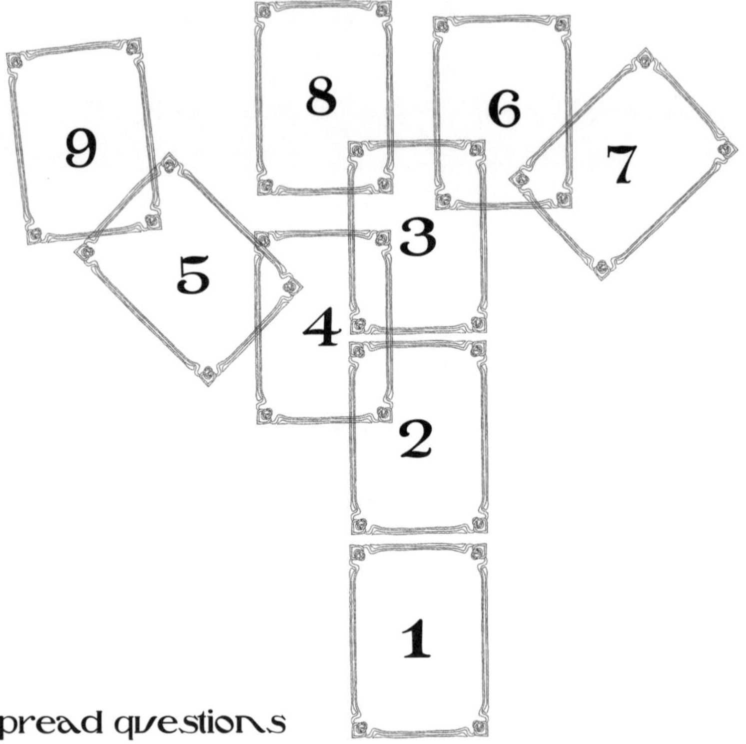

Spread questions

1 - What unknown challenges await me on my next journey?
2 - What fears must I confront to move forward?
3 - What hidden strengths can guide me through this darkness?
4 - What source of hope or inspiration keeps me moving forward?
5 - Who or what provides unexpected support in times of need?
6 - What important lessons can I learn from my current struggles?
7 - What illusions must I see through to reach clarity?
8 - How can I transform challenges into opportunities for growth?
9 - What positive outcomes await me at the end of this journey?

Date: ....../....../......

I embrace renewed love, awakening joy and deepening heartfelt connections.

....

What deck called to me to be used today?

....

What is my own interpretation of each card?

....

....

....

....

....

....

....

....

....

....

....

....

....

How does this reading inspire me to take action?

....

....

Most prominent shadow this reading?

....

Challenges I have surmounted	**Fears I've faced**
....	....
....	....
....	....
....	....
....	....

Gillikin Country

In Gillikin Country, wisdom and intuition emerge as guiding beacons, illuminating the unknown terrains of our inner selves. This mystical land reveals the silent, often unnoticed insights that guide our decisions and perceptions.

The spreads in this section are crafted to delve into the depths of your intuitive wisdom, reflecting on the subtle truths that help navigate your journey. Explore how these insights can illuminate your path and enhance personal clarity.

Lion: "I would be brave if I only had courage."

Gillikin Country
Tarot Challenge

Pick one question and one card each morning for ten days.
Reflect upon the meaning and journal your thoughts in the evening.

- What intuitive message seeks my attention right now?
- How can I cultivate a deeper connection to my inner wisdom?
- What signs or symbols guide my current journey?
- How do past insights inform my present decisions?
- In what areas can I rely more on my intuition?
- What practices enhance my ability to listen to inner wisdom?
- How does intuition illuminate my path forward?
- Who in my life embodies wisdom I can learn from?
- How can I honour the intuitive gifts within me?
- What affirmation can I create to nurture my wisdom daily?

Scarecrow: "I have an idea for a plan."

Path of Inner Wisdom

This spread aligns like a compass, symbolising inner guidance towards true direction. Each card reveals paths illuminated by wisdom, echoing the Gillikins' insightful nature.

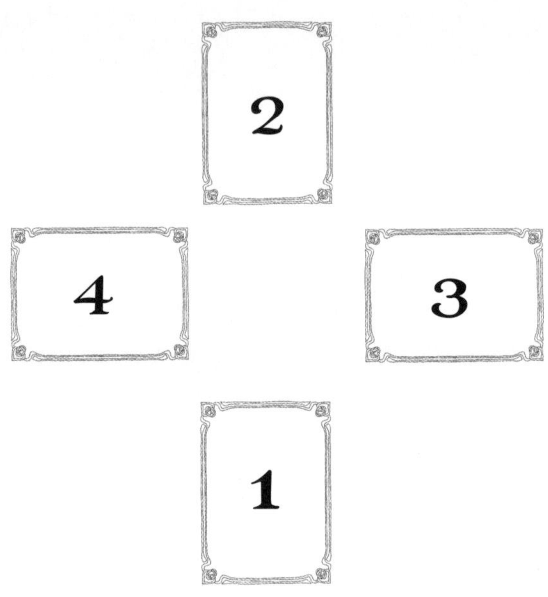

Spread questions

1 - What direction does my inner compass suggest?

2 - Where does my true self feel led?

3 - What insights illuminate my way forward?

4 - How does wisdom shape my path today?

Date: ....../....../......

My inner compass guides me with wisdom and clarity.

....

What deck called to me to be used today?

....

What is my own interpretation of each card?

....

....

....

....

....

....

....

....

....

....

....

....

....

How does this reading inspire me to take action?

....

....

Most prominent lesson I've become aware of this reading?

....

Reflective thoughts & feelings	Elemental influence
....	....
....	....
....	....
....	....
....	....

Intuitive Insights

This spread unfolds as rippling streams, symbolising flowing intuition guiding decisions. Each card encourages intuitive understanding, reflecting Gillikin's deep-seated knowledge.

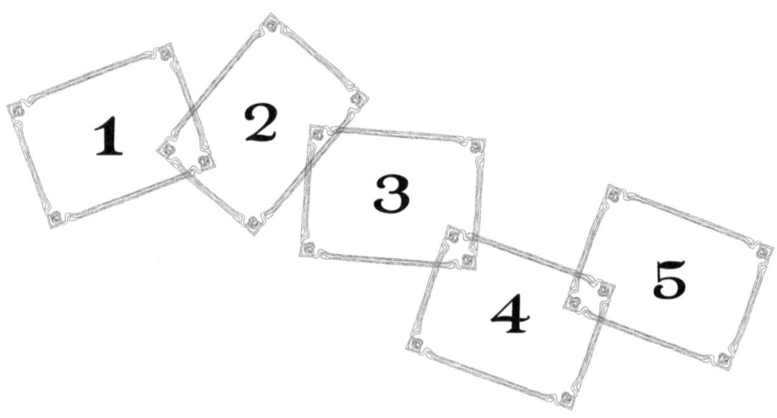

Spread questions

1 - What intuitive stream should I follow now?

2 - How can I deepen my intuitive understanding?

3 - What source of wisdom guides my decisions?

Extended spread questions

4 - How do I trust my intuition to make choices?

5 - Where is my intuition directing me?

Date: ....../....../......

I trust my intuition, letting it guide my choices confidently.

....

What deck called to me to be used today?

....

What is my own interpretation of each card?

....

....

....

....

....

....

....

....

....

....

....

....

....

How does this reading inspire me to take action?

....

....

Most prominent lesson I've become aware of this reading?

....

Reflective thoughts & feelings	Elemental influence
....	....
....	....
....	....
....	....
....	....

Guiding Stars

This spread maps out like the night sky, symbolising navigation by intuitive insight. Each card lights the way with wisdom, echoing the Gillikins' mystical guidance.

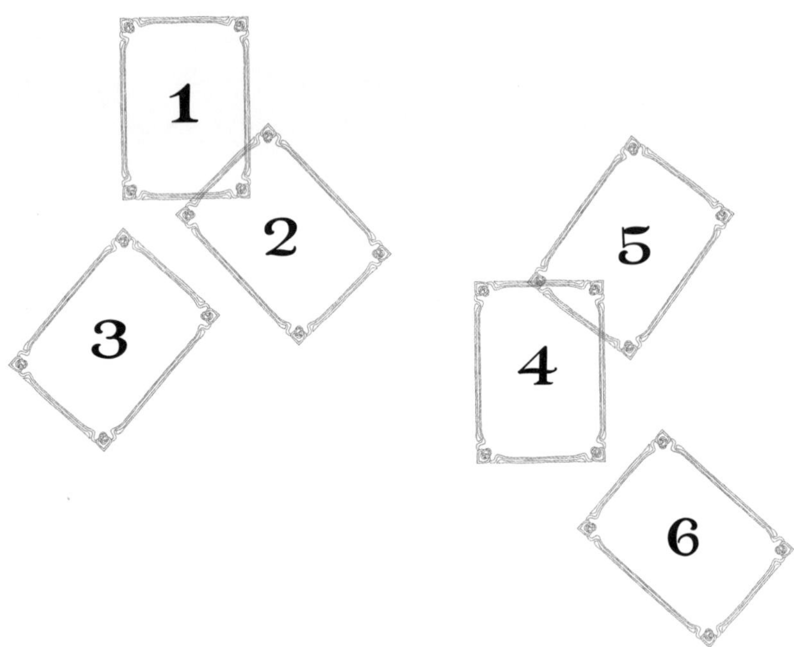

Spread questions

1 - What do the stars reveal about my direction?
2 - How do intuitive insights guide my journey?
3 - Which star offers the wisdom I need?

Extended spread questions

4 - What Gillikin insight shines brightest for me now?
5 - How do universal energies of Oz steer me?
6 - How does this clarity illuminate my path?

Date: ....../....../......

Guiding stars of intuition illuminate my path with wisdom.

....

What deck called to me to be used today?

....

What is my own interpretation of each card?

....

....

....

....

....

....

....

....

....

....

....

....

....

How does this reading inspire me to take action?

....

....

Most prominent lesson I've become aware of this reading?

....

Reflective thoughts & feelings	Elemental influence
....	....
....	....
....	....
....	....
....	....

Whispers of the North

Arranged like swirling northern lights, this spread symbolises receiving and understanding subtle messages. Each card captures delicate insights, reflecting the Gillikins' wisdom.

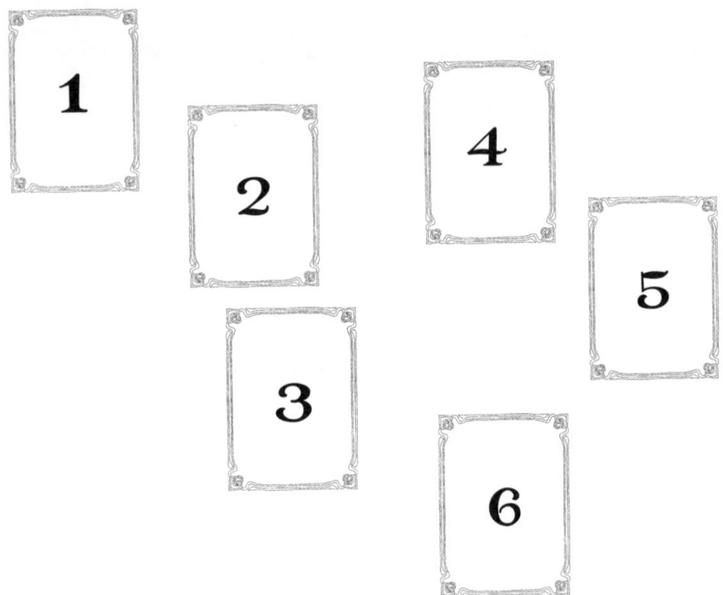

Spread questions

1 - What subtle messages am I receiving?

2 - How do I comprehend these whispers of wisdom?

3 - What gentle insight needs my attention at this time?

Extended spread questions

4 - Where do the northern whispers of my subconscious lead?

5 - How can I best hear the whispers of wisdom?

6 - What does my inner wisdom whisper to me?

Date: ....../....../......

I hear the whispers of wisdom, guiding me from within.

What deck called to me to be used today?

What is my own interpretation of each card?

How does this reading inspire me to take action?

Most prominent lesson I've become aware of this reading?

Reflective thoughts & feelings

Elemental influence

Mystic Vision

This spread is laid like a seer's eye, symbolising visions gained through intuitive clarity. Each card unveils insights, echoing the mystical nature of Gillikin Country.

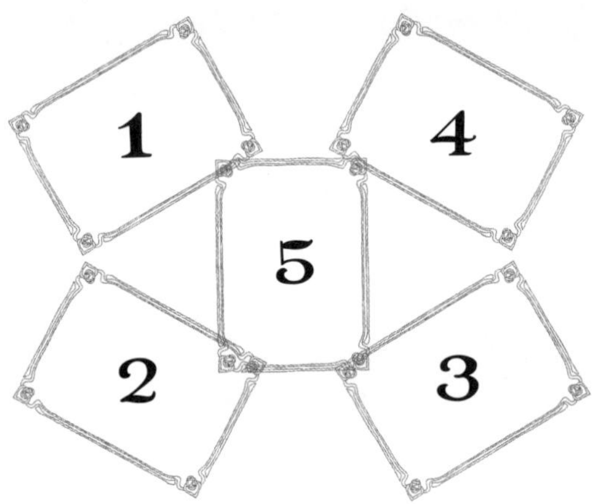

Spread questions

1 - What mystical visions should I pay attention to?
2 - How do these visions shape my understanding?
3 - What does the Gillikin mysticism reveal to me?
4 - How do my visions and dreams guide my intuitive clarity?
5 - What is the impact of intuitive insight on my path?

Date: ....../....../......

I see clearly, with vision shaped and guided by my own intuitive insight.

What deck called to me to be used today?

What is my own interpretation of each card?

How does this reading inspire me to take action?

Most prominent lesson I've become aware of this reading?

Reflective thoughts & feelings

Elemental influence

Clarity's Journey

This spread arcs like a bright dawn, symbolising the journey towards mental clarity. Each card deepens personal awareness and understanding, just like Gillikin's wisdom.

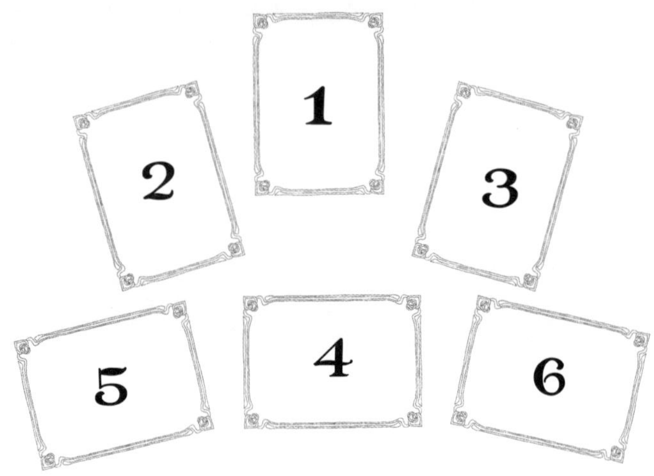

Spread questions

1 - What clear understanding emerges along my journey?
2 - How can clarity purify my thoughts?
3 - Where does wisdom shine brightest for me?

Extended spread questions

4 - What elements of my life guide me towards clarity?
5 - How do I deepen my awareness through this journey of self?
6 - Where is my journey towards clarity leading me?

Date: ....../....../......

I see clearly, clarity and wisdom light my journey, purifying my thoughts.

....

What deck called to me to be used today?

....

What is my own interpretation of each card?

....

....

....

....

....

....

....

....

....

....

....

....

....

How does this reading inspire me to take action?

....

....

Most prominent lesson I've become aware of this reading?

....

Reflective thoughts & feelings

....

....

....

....

....

Elemental influence

....

....

....

....

....

Mindful Guidance

This spread is laid as guiding steps, symbolising mindful learning through guidance. Each card offers wisdom and insight, echoing the lessons of the Gillikins.

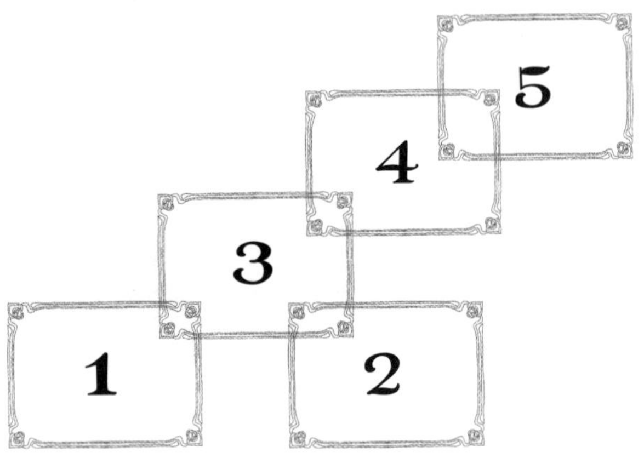

Spread questions

1 - What mindful lesson am I encountering now?

2 - How can I apply this guidance with each step?

3 - What insightful learning will yield the most wisdom?

4 - How do I begin to grow with mindful intent?

5 - Which steps align with deepest understanding?

Date: ....../....../......

I am mindful and move forward with wisdom, learning each step as I go.

What deck called to me to be used today?

What is my own interpretation of each card?

How does this reading inspire me to take action?

Most prominent lesson I've become aware of this reading?

Reflective thoughts & feelings

Elemental influence

Mystical Pathways

This spread weaves like connecting threads of fate, symbolising pathways of mystical understanding. Each card reveals hidden truths, channelled by the mystic energy of the Gillikins.

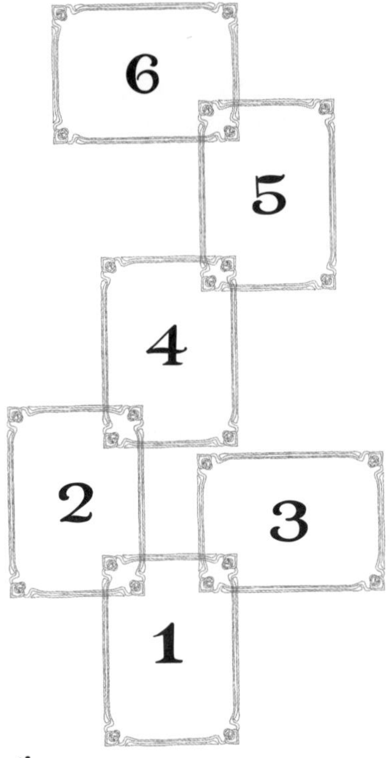

Spread questions

1 - What new mystical connections are emerging for me?

2 - Where do hidden truths guide my journey?

3 - How does mystical energy influence my daily decisions?

4 - What insights come to me through mystical channels?

Extended spread questions

5 - Where do these mystical pathways lead?

6 - In what ways does mysticism reveal life's truths to me?

Date: ....../....../......

I am open to mystical pathways and hidden truths guiding my life's journey.

What deck called to me to be used today?

What is my own interpretation of each card?

How does this reading inspire me to take action?

Most prominent lesson I've become aware of this reading?

Reflective thoughts & feelings

Elemental influence

Inner Guide

This spread orbits like a guiding planet, symbolising the pull of internal guidance. Each card enhances self-trust and understanding, echoing Gillikin Country's cosmic essence.

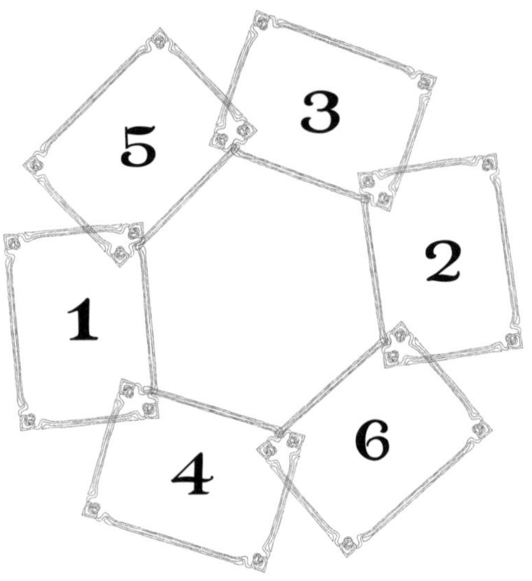

Spread questions

1 - What pulls me toward inner understanding?
2 - How do I nurture my trust in guidance from others?
3 - What about my own inner guidance leads me forward?
4 - How does my inner guide enhance my self-awareness?

Extended spread questions

5 - What is the true essence of my inner guidance?
6 - Where does my true inner guide wish to steer me in this life?

Date: ....../....../......

I navigate my life with ease, and I trust my inner guide to steer me true.

What deck called to me to be used today?

What is my own interpretation of each card?

How does this reading inspire me to take action?

Most prominent lesson I've become aware of this reading?

Reflective thoughts & feelings

Elemental influence

North Star Wisdom

This spread shines like a radiant star, symbolising unwavering directional wisdom. Each card offers guiding insights, reflecting true northern knowledge.

Spread questions

1 - What wisdom does my inner star shine upon?

2 - How is my direction unwavering in wisdom?

3 - What insights are reflected by my guiding star?

4 - Where is my ever-constant north pointing me now?

Date: ....../....../......

I am unwavering. My path is brightened by my ever-constant north star.

What deck called to me to be used today?

What is my own interpretation of each card?

How does this reading inspire me to take action?

Most prominent lesson I've become aware of this reading?

Reflective thoughts & feelings

Elemental influence

This spread sails like open seas, symbolising a journey navigated by strong intuition. Each card harnesses intuitive currents, echoing the Gillikin's intuitive guidance.

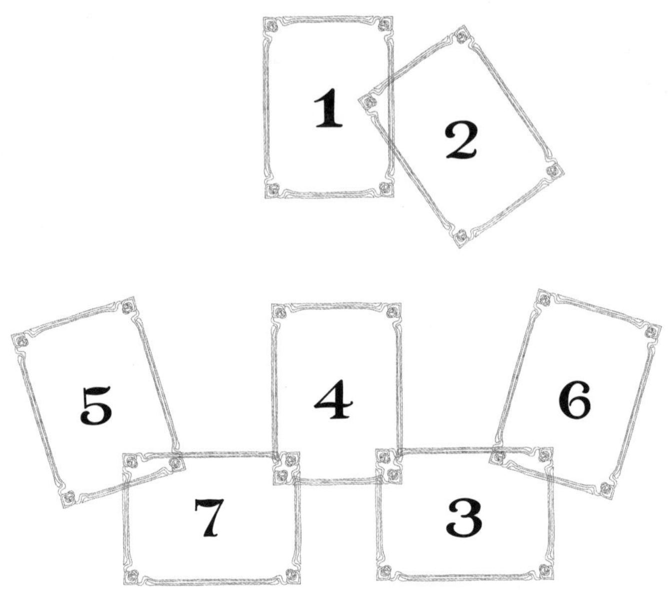

Spread questions

1 - What intuitive currents should I harness?

2 - How does intuition navigate my life's voyage?

3 - Where do intuitive waves guide my path?

Extended spread questions

4 - What insights deepen my understanding and insights?

5 - How do I trust tides of intuition that flow into me?

6 - How is my path mapped by deep knowing?

7 - Where can I anchor with insight and understanding?

Date: ....../....../......

Openly I journey on intuition, navigating life's sea with insight and valour.

....

What deck called to me to be used today?

....

What is my own interpretation of each card?

....

....

....

....

....

....

....

....

....

....

....

....

....

How does this reading inspire me to take action?

....

....

Most prominent lesson I've become aware of this reading?

....

Reflective thoughts & feelings	Elemental influence
....	....
....	....
....	....
....	....
....	....

Illuminated Thoughts

This spread shines like a lit lantern, symbolising thoughts brightened by understanding. Each card deepens insight, reflecting Gillikin wisdom's light.

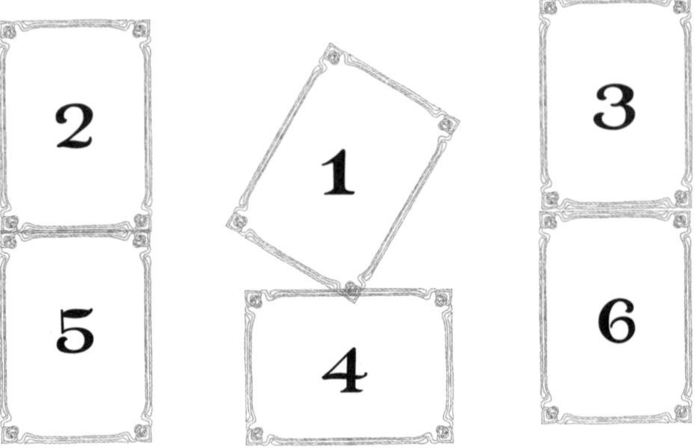

Spread questions

1 - How do my thoughts become illuminated?

2 - What understanding shines brightly?

3 - Which lantern of life lights my thoughtful journeys?

Extended spread questions

4 - How is clarity achieved in my thoughts?

5 - Where does my wisdom reveal new knowledge to me?

6 - How do these insights enlighten and focus] my thinking?

Date: ....../....../......

My thoughts are illuminated and charged by wisdom, faith and understanding.

....

What deck called to me to be used today?

....

What is my own interpretation of each card?

....

....

....

....

....

....

....

....

....

....

....

....

....

How does this reading inspire me to take action?

....

....

Most prominent lesson I've become aware of this reading?

....

Reflective thoughts & feelings	Elemental influence
....	....
....	....
....	....
....	....
....	....

Radiant Self

This spread frames like a mirror, symbolising reflection grounded in profound wisdom. Each card offers reflective insights, inspired by Gillikin's intuitive contemplation.

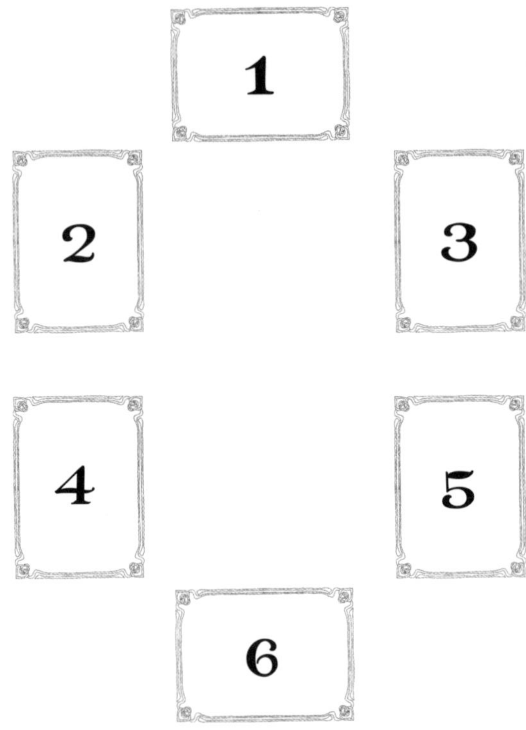

Spread questions

1 - What part of me radiates positively that I don't recognise?

2 - Why do I overlook this radiance?

3 - How can I start to embrace this part of me?

Extended spread questions

4 - What aspect can I nurture to shine brighter in my life?

5 - How can I express my true self in my interactions?

6 - What change will this bring?

Date: ....../....../......

I reflect on life with wisdom and insightful thought, and my true self shines.

....

What deck called to me to be used today?

....

What is my own interpretation of each card?

....

....

....

....

....

....

....

....

....

....

....

....

....

How does this reading inspire me to take action?

....

....

Most prominent lesson I've become aware of this reading?

....

Reflective thoughts & feelings	Elemental influence
....	....
....	....
....	....
....	....
....	....

Beacon of Insight

This spread burns like a lighthouse, symbolising insight that guides through darkness. Each card sheds light on dilemmas, echoing the wisdom of the Gillikins.

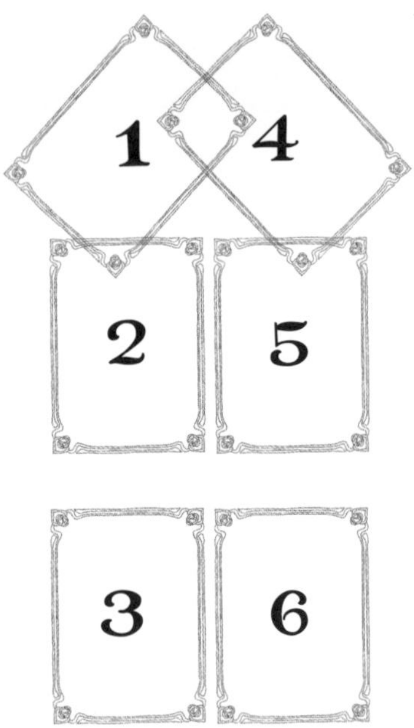

Spread questions

1 - How does insight guide me through darkness?
2 - What light illuminates my current challenges?
3 - How is insight shedding light on dilemmas?

Extended spread questions

4 - How do I gain clarity amid uncertainty?
5 - What beacon directs me toward understanding?
6 - How does wisdom lead me through difficult times?

Date: ....../....../......

I am confident, insight lights my way, guiding me through uncertainty.

....

What deck called to me to be used today?

....

What is my own interpretation of each card?

....

....

....

....

....

....

....

....

....

....

....

....

....

How does this reading inspire me to take action?

....

....

Most prominent lesson I've become aware of this reading?

....

Reflective thoughts & feelings	Elemental influence
....	....
....	....
....	....
....	....
....	....

Council of Inner Wisdom

Echoing the wisdom of the Gillikins, this spread marks a circle of advisors, symbolising inner voices of wisdom. Each card tapping into self-knowing guidance.

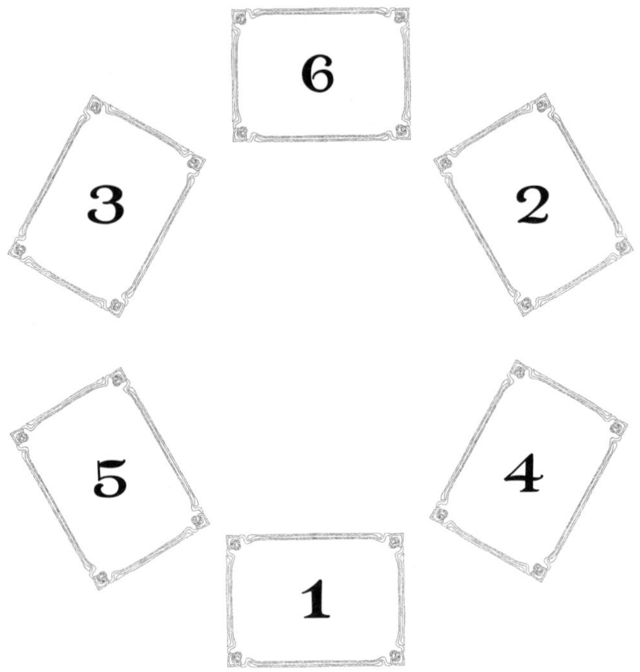

Spread questions

1 - Which inner voices provide wisdom today?

2 - What did the council reveal to me to guide my actions?

3 - How do I begin to better engage with my inner dialogues?

Extended spread questions

4 - How does self-knowing direct my steps?

5 - What wisdom circulates within me?

6 - How does my inner council guide me toward mindful action?

Date: ....../....../......

My inner council of wisdom always leads me toward mindful action and beliefs.

What deck called to me to be used today?

What is my own interpretation of each card?

How does this reading inspire me to take action?

Most prominent lesson I've become aware of this reading?

Reflective thoughts & feelings

Elemental influence

This spread illuminates the path toward leaving a meaningful and prosperous legacy.The layout resembles a golden goblet, a radiant vessel symbolising potential, success, and the vibrant life force energy that propels your legacy into being.

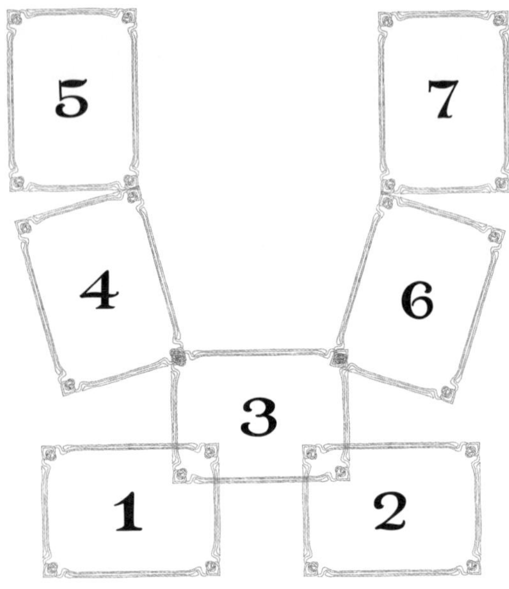

Spread questions

1 - What new understanding dawns on my path?

2 - How does each step enlighten my way?

3 - What bright insights illuminate my journey?

Extended spread questions

4 - How do enlightenment and understanding align in my life?

5 - Where does the light guide with wisdom?

6 - What pathways does wisdom guide me through?

7 - How does wisdom continually light and support my journey?

Date: ....../....../......

My journey is enlightened by learned wisdom at every turn and step.

....

What deck called to me to be used today?

....

What is my own interpretation of each card?

....

....

....

....

....

....

....

....

....

....

....

....

....

How does this reading inspire me to take action?

....

....

Most prominent lesson I've become aware of this reading?

....

Reflective thoughts & feelings	Elemental influence
....	....
....	....
....	....
....	....
....	....

In the mystical Land of Purple, the Gillikins guide you to pull a card, this represents your greatest gift of wisdom in your life. Allow the card's revelations to illuminate your path as you spend 10 minutes in a quiet place, meditating. Write down any thoughts or feelings that arise during this time.

Tin Woodman: "My greatest wish is to be alive."

Date: ....../....../......

I trust my intuition, guided by inner wisdom through life's unfolding mysteries.

What is the greatest gift of wisdom this tarot card communicates to you?

In what areas of your life can this new wisdom illuminate your path forward?

How has your intuition shaped your decisions in the past?

How can you harness this wisdom to enhance your life and choices?

Create an affirmation that encapsulates the wisdom of this card.

Emotions during meditation

Channelled insights

Quadling Country

Quadling Country celebrates love as the cornerstone of fulfillment, reflecting the power of gratitude and connection in enriching our lives. Here, love's resilience often unveils truths about our deepest desires and connections.

The spreads in this section are designed to embrace the nurturing essence of love, prompting reflection on how appreciation and connection enhance your journey. Discover how cultivating love and gratitude can lead to profound personal fulfillment and joy.

Tin Man: "You are in luck to not have a heart."

Quadling Country Tarot Challenge

Pick one question and one card each morning for ten days. Reflect upon the meaning and journal your thoughts in the evening.

- How does love currently manifest in my life?
- What relationships deserve deeper gratitude and appreciation?
- How can I nurture loving connections more authentically?
- What past event taught me the value of real love?
- How does self-love shape my interactions with others?
- What fulfillment comes from embracing gratitude daily?
- How can I express appreciation to those who matter?
- What role does love play in assisting me achieving my goals?
- How does love empower me to be my best self?
- What loving affirmation can guide my daily interactions?

Scarecrow: "I have an idea for a plan."

Glinda's Guidance

This spread shines like Glinda's spell that symbolises love's guiding wisdom. Each card channels wisdom and care, reflecting Glinda's role in Dorothy's journey.

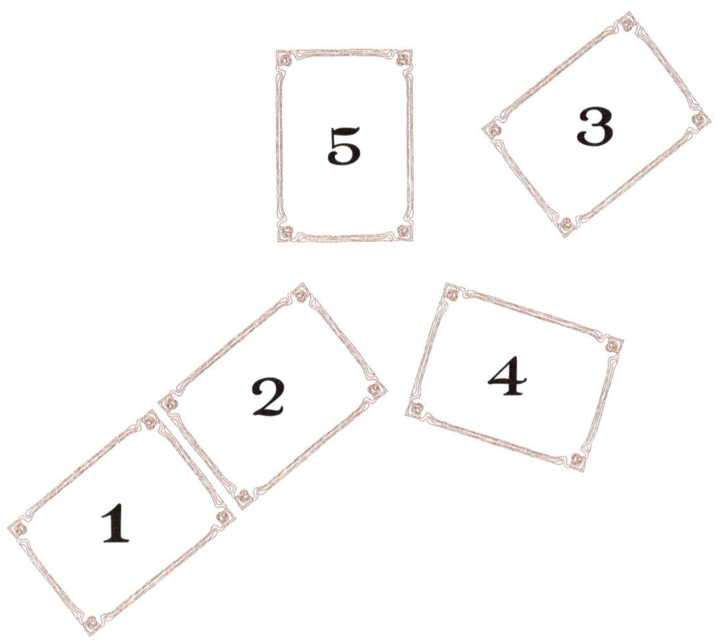

Spread questions

1 - What supportive guidance is present in my life?

2 - How am I shielded by love?

3 - What does my heart truly seek?

4 - Where does happiness lead me?

5 - Who do I need to thank for guidance?

Date: ....../....../......

I am love, I am loved, I am guided by love, I find harmony in every step.

....

What deck called to me to be used today?

....

What is my own interpretation of each card?

....

....

....

....

....

....

....

....

....

....

....

....

....

How does this reading inspire me to take action?

....

....

Most prominent lesson I've become aware of this reading?

....

Reflective thoughts & feelings	Elemental influence
....	....
....	....
....	....
....	....
....	....

The Silver Slippers

Laid as a shimmering silver slipper, this spread embodies Dorothy's quest. Each card reflects steps in finding home and love akin to the silver slippers' promise.

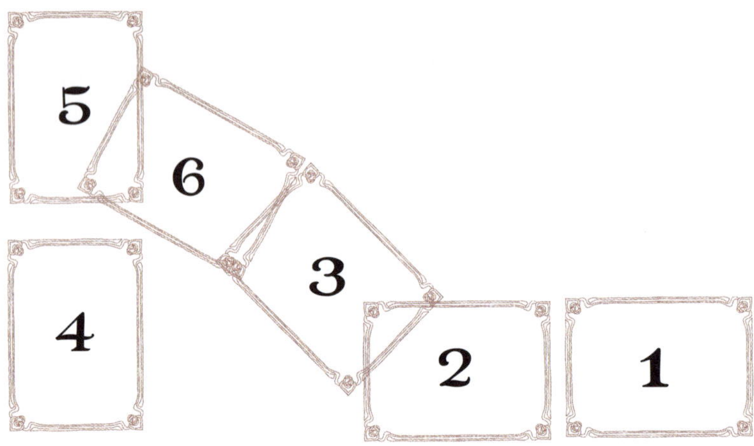

Spread questions

1 - What quest brings me closest to home within myself?

2 - Where am I currently on my path to joy?

3 - What love must I cherish?

Extended spread

4 - What do I need to accomplish for peace?

5 - How does gratitude shape my journey?

6 - Where do I feel most complete?

Date: ....../....../......

I am following my destined path. The path home is love and my steps are joyful.

....

What deck called to me to be used today?

....

What is my own interpretation of each card?

....

....

....

....

....

....

....

....

....

....

....

....

....

How does this reading inspire me to take action?

....

....

Most prominent lesson I've become aware of this reading?

....

Reflective thoughts & feelings	Elemental influence
....	....
....	....
....	....
....	....
....	....

Scarecrow's Wisdom

Laid as a wise and curious brain, this spread signposts insight and wisdom. Inspired by Scarecrow, each card provides direction through cleverness and clarity.

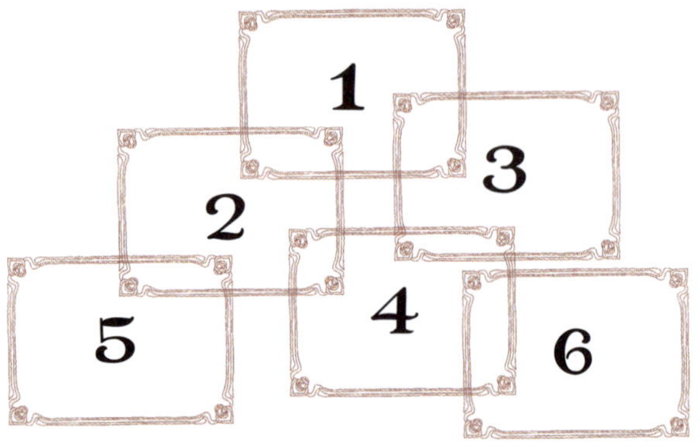

Spread questions

1 - What insight sharpens my focus?

2 - Who shares the journey of discovery?

3 - How can mutual wisdom aid my path?

4 - What knowledge lights my way?

Extended spread

5 - What intellectual tool solves my issues?

6 - Where do insights guide me?

Date: ....../....../......

I am focused. Insight and clarity light my path with Scarecrow's wisdom.

....

What deck called to me to be used today?

....

What is my own interpretation of each card?

....

....

....

....

....

....

....

....

....

....

....

....

....

How does this reading inspire me to take action?

....

....

Most prominent lesson I've become aware of this reading?

....

Reflective thoughts & feelings

....

....

....

....

....

Elemental influence

....

....

....

....

....

Field of Poppies

Laid like an awakening poppy bloom, this spread highlights invigorating love. Each card propels you toward renewed vitality, echoing Dorothy's fight through the enchanted field.

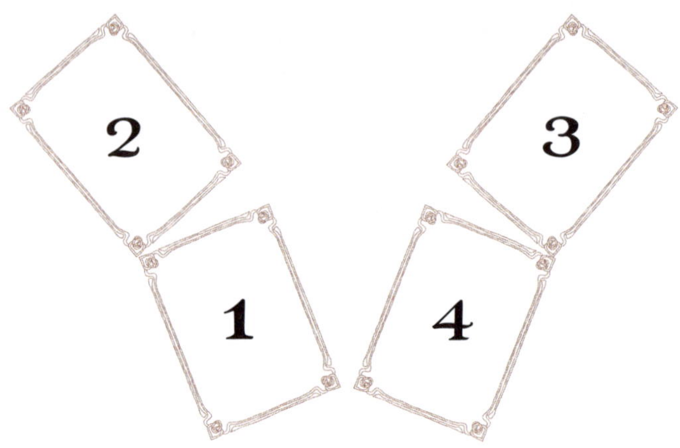

Spread questions

1 - What stirs and awakens me from stagnation?
2 - Where do I find new vitality and rejuvenation?
3 - What type of love energises my actions?
4 - How do I maintain healthy momentum in my relationships?

Date: ....../....../......

Love invigorates me, renewed vitality lifts me beyond stagnation's field.

What deck called to me to be used today?

What is my own interpretation of each card?

How does this reading inspire me to take action?

Most prominent lesson I've become aware of this reading?

Reflective thoughts & feelings

Elemental influence

Dorothy and Friends

Interlinked with fingers laced like Dorothy's circle of friends, this spread fosters love and loyalty. Each card honours affectionate ties within a friendship circle.

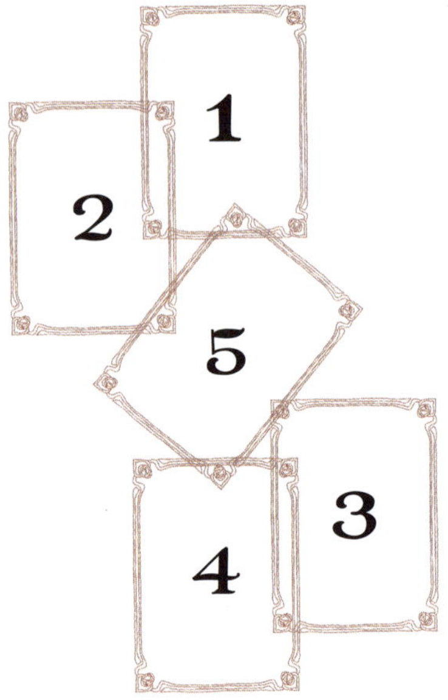

Spread questions

1 - Where does true loyalty flourish in my friendships?

2 - What heartfelt connection strengthens my group bonds?

3 - How are affections demonstrated within my friend group?

4 - Who is my network of strong support?

5 - What joyous moment or memories bind us together?

Date: ....../....../......

I am a friend to all. Friendship's joy binds us in laughter and loyalty.

What deck called to me to be used today?

What is my own interpretation of each card?

How does this reading inspire me to take action?

Most prominent lesson I've become aware of this reading?

Reflective thoughts & feelings

Elemental influence

Ozma's Blessing

Flowing like a royal canopy of flowers, this spread bestows blessings of love to all. Each card channels Ozma's royal grace into everyday acts and blessings.

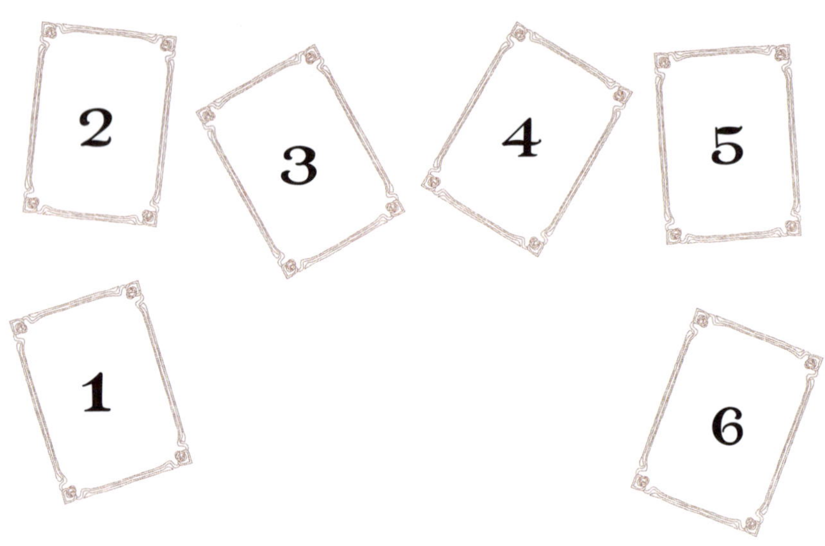

Spread questions

1 - What unexpected blessings are about to appear for me?
2 - Where do I feel honoured in love?
3 - What deed earns thanks and reverence?

Extended spread

4 - Who stands by me earnestly?
5 - Where do new blessings direct my path?
6 - What love endures as my greatest legacy?

Date: ....../....../......

I cherish all the blessings in my day, I am crowned by love and grace.

What deck called to me to be used today?

What is my own interpretation of each card?

How does this reading inspire me to take action?

Most prominent lesson I've become aware of this reading?

Reflective thoughts & feelings

Elemental influence

Tin Man's Love

This spread is laid to represent Tin Man's compassionate heart, this spread spreads love and warmth. Each card opens pathways to healing and all-encompassing love.

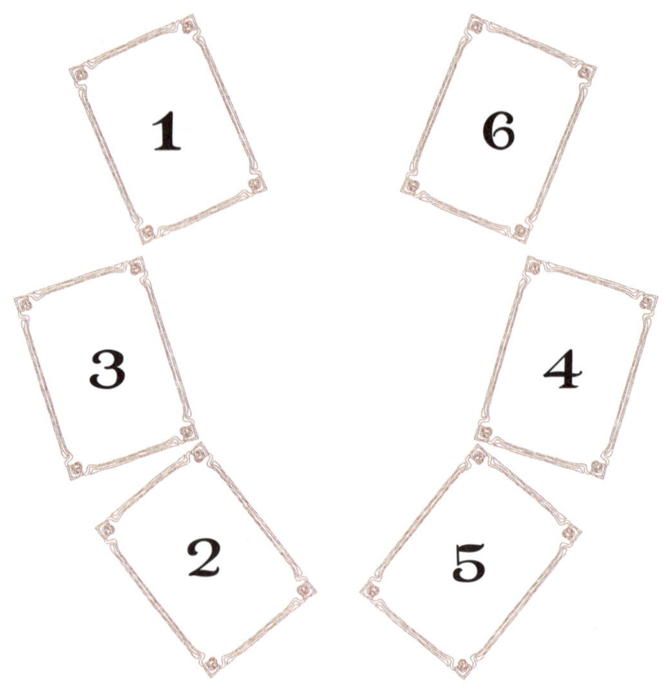

Spread questions

1 - What opens my heart to let love into my life?

2 - What makes me feel compassion deeply?

3 - How do I nurture warmth and kindness toward myself?

Extended spread

4 - Where is empathy most needed in my life?

5 - What acts can repair broken affections?

6 - How do I embody love in order to how compassion?

Date: ....../....../......

I have empathy. Compassion fills my heart. I am pure of heart and mind.

What deck called to me to be used today?

What is my own interpretation of each card?

How does this reading inspire me to take action?

Most prominent lesson I've become aware of this reading?

Reflective thoughts & feelings

Elemental influence

Emerald City Light

Symbolising the radiant vista of the Emerald City, this spread illuminates bright engagements in life. Each card resonates with insights of love fulfilled.

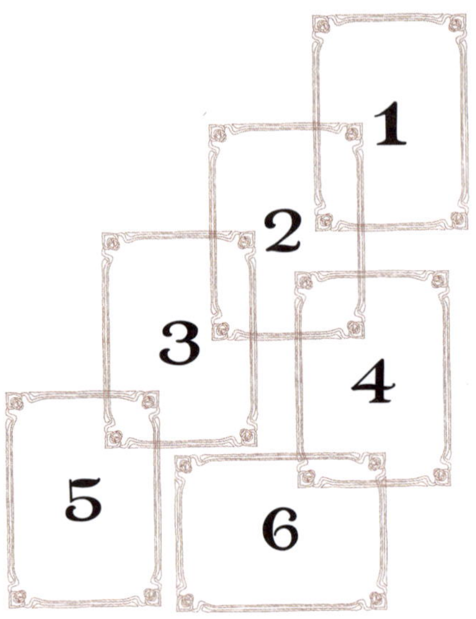

Spread questions

1 - What brings me brightness and lights up my world?

2 - Where does love's glow spark affection?

3 - Who propels my joy and engagement?

4 - What guides me and illuminates darkened thoughts?

5 - Where do heartfelt epiphanies arise?

6 - How does love steer future fulfillment for a brighter tomorrow?

Date: ....../....../......

Love's radiance brightens my journey, illuminating fulfilment and pleasures.

What deck called to me to be used today?

What is my own interpretation of each card?

How does this reading inspire me to take action?

Most prominent lesson I've become aware of this reading?

Reflective thoughts & feelings

Elemental influence

Nurturing Circle

This spread emulates Glinda's embrace, this spread encircles nurturing connections. Each card encourages cultivating care and inclusivity embraced openly.

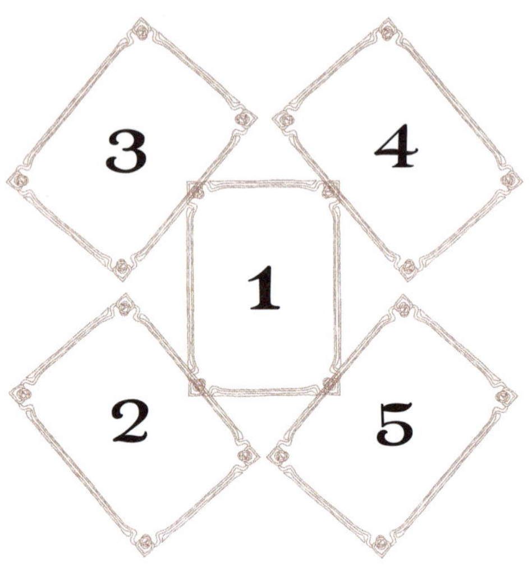

Spread questions

1 - How do I welcome acceptance and love into my days?
2 - Where does kindness need cultivating and nurturing?
3 - Who benefits from my open-hearted warmth?
4 - What new engagements will foster personal growth?
5 - Where should I nurture bonds so my loving acts flourish?

Date: ....../....../......

I nourish inclusivity, embracing love through openness, honesty and integrity.

What deck called to me to be used today?

What is my own interpretation of each card?

How does this reading inspire me to take action?

Most prominent lesson I've become aware of this reading?

Reflective thoughts & feelings

Elemental influence

Glinda's Gratitude

With gracious deeds like acts of kindness, this spread inspires gratitude. Laid in the shape of pressed palms, each card bestows recognition upon gracious acts meriting heartfelt thanks.

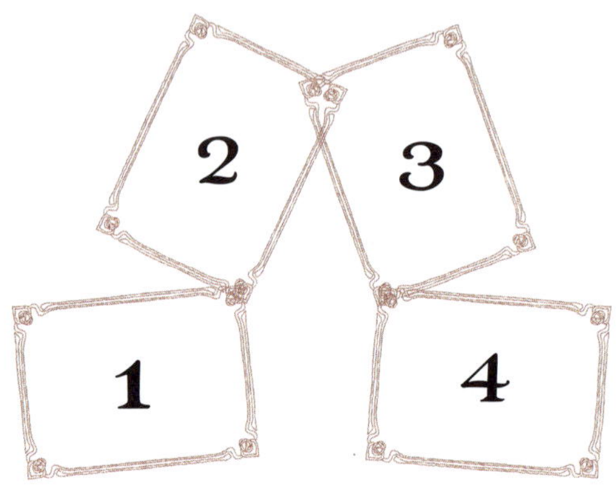

Spread questions

1 - What gift of thanks will honour gracious deeds I have done?
2 - How does this recognition serve to improve my loving acts?
3 - Who in my life acts with grace deserving my gratitude?
4 - What graciousness must I always cherish?

Date: ....../....../......

I give with love, and my gracious deeds earn gratitude, felt warmly and sincerely.

What deck called to me to be used today?

What is my own interpretation of each card?

How does this reading inspire me to take action?

Most prominent lesson I've become aware of this reading?

Reflective thoughts & feelings

Elemental influence

Path of Love

Interwoven like a blanket of love, this spread highlights united steps taken together. Each card fosters companionship and togetherness, honouring both destination and destiny.

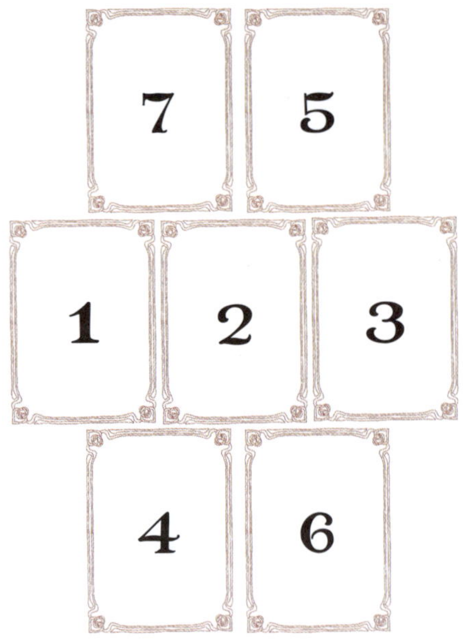

Spread questions

1 - Who walks my loving path?
2 - What signs can remind me of such affection today?
3 - Where do our love-led paths intersect?

Extended spread questions

4 - How can shared love foster deeper journeying together?
5 - What signs of growth appear within love's embrace?
6 - What road will lead me to loving fulfilment?
7 - Where does love's journey end for this connection?

Date: ....../....../......

I am part of the whole, and love guides our journey, shared in unity and grace.

What deck called to me to be used today?

What is my own interpretation of each card?

How does this reading inspire me to take action?

Most prominent lesson I've become aware of this reading?

Reflective thoughts & feelings

Elemental influence

Courage on the Road

Crafted like Tin Man's shield, this spread depicts how you protect love with courage. Each card represents acts displaying bravery, honourably reflecting affection.

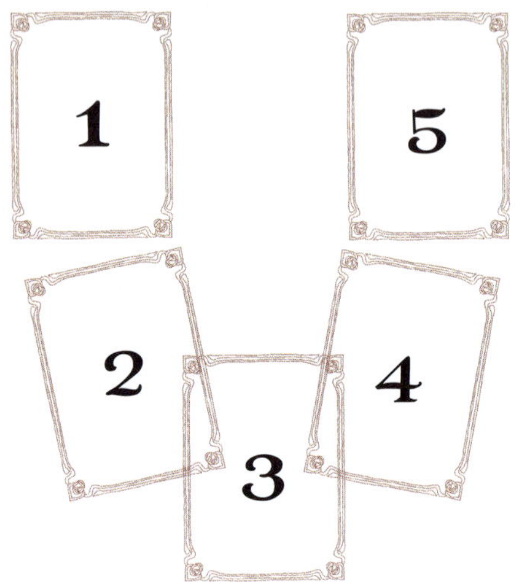

Spread questions

1 - What strengthens and emboldens my affectionate heart?

2 - How does courteousness empower affection?

3 - Where is boldness reflected in bonds I have with others?

4 - What strengthens me on love's path?

5 - What brave act must I reveal to be courageous?

Date: ....../....../......

I am fearless in love. Love's bravery propels my path with heartfelt strength.

What deck called to me to be used today?

What is my own interpretation of each card?

How does this reading inspire me to take action?

Most prominent lesson I've become aware of this reading?

Reflective thoughts & feelings

Elemental influence

Wise Companions

Emulating Scarecrow's crown and influence as king, this spread thrives on close bonds and their wisdom. Each card acknowledges learning, and aids in cultivating insightful and cognitive growth.

Spread questions

1 - What insightful exchanges enrich my learning experience?
2 - What life lessons are best gathered collectively?
3 - How do friendships enhance my understanding of life?
4 - What intelligence do we share in our community?
5 - Where does collaboration intensify our shared wisdom?

Date: ....../....../......

I am cherished, and I treasure wisdom gained from the deep bonds of friendship.

What deck called to me to be used today?

What is my own interpretation of each card?

How does this reading inspire me to take action?

Most prominent lesson I've become aware of this reading?

Reflective thoughts & feelings

Elemental influence

Emerald Heart

Laid out as the Emerald City's heart centre, this spread infuses the feeling of reunion. Each card resonates with fulfilled harmony, and flourishing open connections.

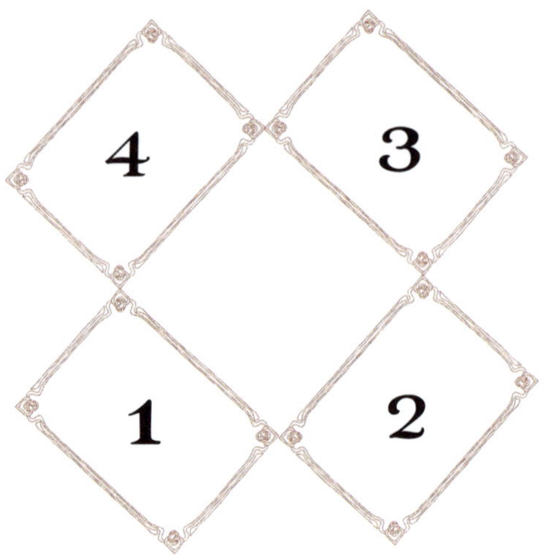

Spread questions

1 - How does my heart rejoice in open love?
2 - What fulfills my heart and encourages affection?
3 - Who or what bridges my desires and dreams?
4 - What unified goal strengthens my destiny's foundation?

Date: ....../....../......

I am complete. Love completes me, uniting my heart, my soul and my dreams.

....

What deck called to me to be used today?

....

What is my own interpretation of each card?

....

....

....

....

....

....

....

....

....

....

....

....

....

How does this reading inspire me to take action?

....

....

Most prominent lesson I've become aware of this reading?

....

Reflective thoughts & feelings

....

....

....

....

....

Elemental influence

....

....

....

....

....

Joyful Laughter

Designed to mirror a beam of playful light, this spread brings merriment, celebrating comfort in joy. Each card fuels laughter, celebrating Dorothy's companions connections, and their cherished hearts.

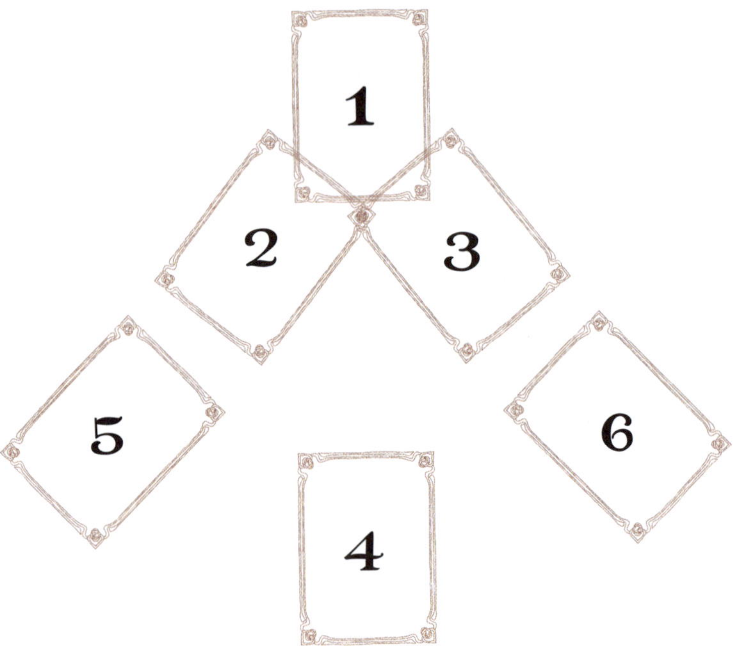

Spread questions

1 - Where can I share genuine laughter?

2 - How does joy brighten my day?

3 - What fun delights my true heart?

Extended spread

4 - What companion joins in my laughter?

5 - What fun activity inspires joy within my soul?

6 - Where does laughter return to me?

Date: ....../....../......

I am the song of laughter in my heart. Laughter's joy fills my days with delight.

....

What deck called to me to be used today?

....

What is my own interpretation of each card?

....

....

....

....

....

....

....

....

....

....

....

....

....

How does this reading inspire me to take action?

....

....

Most prominent lesson I've become aware of this reading?

....

Reflective thoughts & feelings	Elemental influence
....	....
....	....
....	....
....	....
....	....

Circle of Compassion

Encircling like an infinite embrace, this spread unites cohesive love. Each card reflects community and kindness, with feelings of love rooted at every empathetic turn.

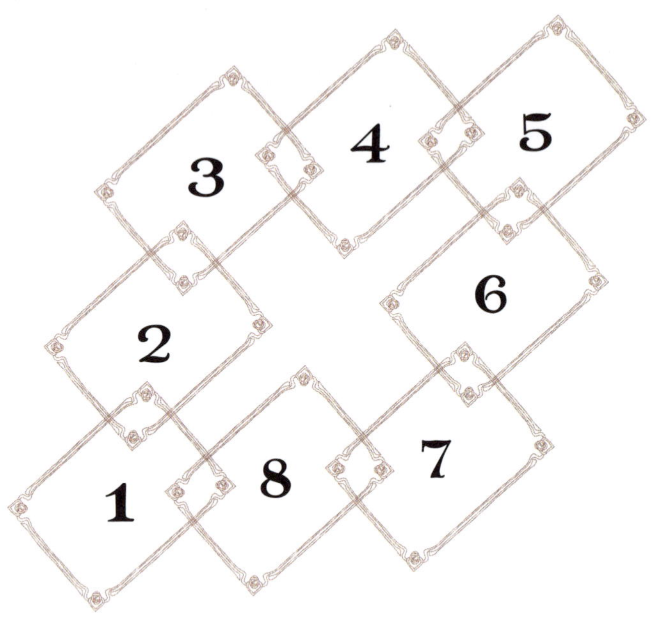

Spread questions

1 - How do I welcome in love's circle?
2 - What loving acts should enrich groups I connect with?
3 - How do shared stories broaden the collective's understanding?
4 - Where does compassion build mutual bonds?

Extended spread questions

5 - How does diversity strengthen my connections?
6 - How can I embrace proximity to others for shared growth?
7 - What shared experiences will refine my love relations?
8 - How do smiles affect and reflect unity in my life?

Date: ....../....../......

I am an infinite circle of self love. Compassion encircles me in a huge love hug.

....

What deck called to me to be used today?

....

What is my own interpretation of each card?

....

....

....

....

....

....

....

....

....

....

....

....

....

How does this reading inspire me to take action?

....

....

Most prominent lesson I've become aware of this reading?

....

Reflective thoughts & feelings	Elemental influence
....	....
....	....
....	....
....	....
....	....

Land Of Red

In the warm embrace of the Land of Red, the Quadlings guide you to draw a card and notice what message of love and gratitude it evokes. Write a letter of appreciation to someone who has supported you, reflecting on how their presence enriches your life. Let the card's essence inspire your words.

Wizard of Oz: "Time is the best healer."

Date: ....../....../......

I am fulfilled by love and gratitude, nurturing my heart's deepest joy.

....

What aspects of the tarot card evoke feelings of love and gratitude?

....

....

How has the person you are writing to been a gift in your life?

....

....

....

....

....

Describe a specific moment when their presence made a significant difference.

....

....

....

....

....

How does this card capture that essence?

....

....

....

Reflect on the emotions that arise when you think of this person.

....

....

Ways in which I show love	How I am loved
....	....
....	....
....	....
....	....
....	....

No Place Like Home

As you conclude your journey with wisdom and insight, connect with the essence of home and grounding. This task invites you to use your tarot deck to explore the nurturing aspects of your life, honouring those who symbolise stability and growth in your life.

Dorothy: "I'm so glad to be at home again!"

Spread questions

1 - **Aunt Em's Anchor Card** symbolises stability and practicality, reflecting the grounding force in your life that offers comfort and security. What is this card asking you to embrace as a reminder of the strong foundation from which you began your journey.

2 - **Dorothy's Reflection Card** embodies curiosity and growth. This card captures the transformative spirit and personal insights gained through your adventures. What is guiding you to reflect on how these lessons influence your path ahead.

3 - **Uncle Henry's Gratitude Card** symbolises resilience and quiet strength. As you draw a card, consider the unwavering support that has aided you through recent challenges and what message this card holds for you going forward.

Date: ....../....../......

I shape my future with courage and imagination, welcoming new adventures.

What aspects of home ground you and offer stability in your life?

How has your journey transformed your understanding of security and comfort?

What insights from your journey will you integrate into your everyday routines?

What new found wisdom guides you in creating a nurturing environment?

What qualities of Aunt Em, Dorothy, or Uncle Henry resonate most with you?

How can you cultivate a sense of gratitude for stability and personal growth?

Lessons I've learned

Gifts I've discovered